AIRCRAFT ARCHIVE
FIGHTERS OF WORLD WAR TWO
VOLUME 2

Contents

A DETAILED COLLECTION OF ORIGINAL SCALE AIRCRAFT DRAWINGS

Introduction

In the first of these volumes we introduced the series of scale drawings with an explanation of their origins and their importance as a permanent record of aircraft shapes, and credited the skills of the draughtsmen involved. This second volume extends the range of types which have been taken from the files of 'Aeromodeller' and 'Scale Models', two of the monthly magazines published by the original Model Aeronautical Press, long since absorbed into Argus Specialist Publications.

Each of the drawings in this selected range of very famous fighters has some special significance for the draughtsmen involved. The Das brothers in Holland were determined to place on record the elusive shape of the Fokker D23 and Pino Dell'Orco in Italy wanted aero enthusiasts to appreciate the clean though asymmetric Macchi C202, while John Alcorn in the USA was absolutely dedicated to the Douglas Boston and Arthur Bentley to the Kingston products, the Hurricane and Tempest. So it goes on . . . Each drawing has its own story, from the classic Fiat CR42 biplane to the wartime urgency of the Heinkel Salamander, the lines of which do great credit to its design team considering the aircraft's extraordinary brief development period.

Some of the draughtsmen chose their subject out of an appreciation for its performance. Geoff Duval, a master pilot in his own right, selected the comparatively little known Yakovlev 9 to bring some recognition to a fighter that matched everything the Axis powers could set against it. Given a Merlin engine it might well have become the finest piston engined fighter of World War II, an honour often ascribed to the North American P-51 Mustang which Pat Lloyd took upon himself to measure from life. The Spitfire is not overlooked: Harry Robinson extended his researches to cover all the marks from prototype to the ultimate.

Another approach is reflected in the Fulmar and the Black Widow, two of Brian Taylor's drawings, which were produced out of frustration from wanting to make true-scale radio control models to an international competition standard yet being unable to locate existing drawings of adequate authority. Brian's own initiative resolved the problem: he produced his own drawings, which were checked and certified for official documentation.

Representing the Luftwaffe, three contrasting Messerschmitts, the 163 rocket fighter, the 262 twin jet fighter-bomber and the 410 intruder come from the prolific aero historian Ian Stair and are complemented by Doug Carrick's Bf 109F, another 'first' to get those elusive panel lines absolutely right.

Each set of plans is a typical example of the skill and dedication applied by an amateur researcher over countless hours of translating measurements and interpreting photographs into a scale drawing which,

'. . . The classic CR42 biplane . . .' ▶

◀ Macchi C202 and P-51D Mustang in NASM Washington, two of the outstanding fighters featured in this volume.

'The Spitfire is not overlooked . . .'

in fact, no manufacturer could ever provide! For it may come as a surprise, but the reality is that the manufacturer's general arrangement drawings have little value in the factories, are rarely accurate in shape or scale and, without exception, illustrate the aeroplane in a stage long since superseded by production variants.

Access to the real thing is the ideal, but how can one measure each panel, check every angle and record all the shapes? It takes a special sort of dedication to undertake such a mammoth task – a museum visit will confirm the enormity of the undertaking.

Demand for accuracy and authenticity originated through the work of James Hay Stevens in 'Aeromodeller'. He was among the first to adopt 1/72nd scale, based on the Imperial measure of one sixth of an inch representing one foot. Opening standards, as set by James Stevens, were taken up through the series of *Aircraft of the Fighting Powers* volumes published by Harborough, once an associated company with MAP. Wartime urgency quickly generated a new breed of detail draughtsman, typified by Harry Cooper and Owen Thetford. After seven volumes and the creation of an *Aircraft Described* series, centred on civil aircraft by Eddie Riding, 1/72nd scale was firmly established, and the fine detail in the drawings reached levels of intricacy to satisfy the most demanding enthusiast – though not for long! Aeromodellers have an insatiable appetite for scale information.

From the immediate postwar years to the present day, the levels of minutiae have soared far beyond the first conceptions. Out of *Aircraft Described* came *Aeroplanes in Outline* and *Famous Biplanes*, and, through forty years of publication in 'Aeromodeller' magazine, a band of skilled contributors built up a series which now comes in book form.

The drawings reflect the individual character of the originator. Each was in its time a labour of love, the fruits of which have been the immense pleasure given to students, collectors and aeromodellers. If by reproduction in this form we commemorate their work permanently, rather than in a transient monthly magazine, then we will have rewarded both the draughtsmen and the reader with a treasure store.

Hawker Hurricane Mk I

Country of origin: Great Britain.
Type: Single-seat, land-based interceptor fighter.
Dimensions: Wing span 40ft 0in *12.19m*; length 31ft 11in *9.73m*; height 13ft 1½in *4.00m*; wing area 257.5 sq ft *23.92m²*.
Weights: Empty 4670lb *2119kg*; normal

loaded 6600lb *2995kg*.
Powerplant: One Rolls-Royce Merlin II or III V12, liquid-cooled piston engine rated at 1030hp.
Performance: Maximum speed 330mph *531kph* at 17,500ft *5335m*; initial climb rate 2300ft/min *700m/min*; service

ceiling 36,000ft *10,950m*; range (clean) 425 miles *684km*.
Armament: Eight fixed 0.303in Browning machine guns.
Service: First flight (prototype) 6 November 1935, (Mk I) 12 October 1937; service entry December 1937.

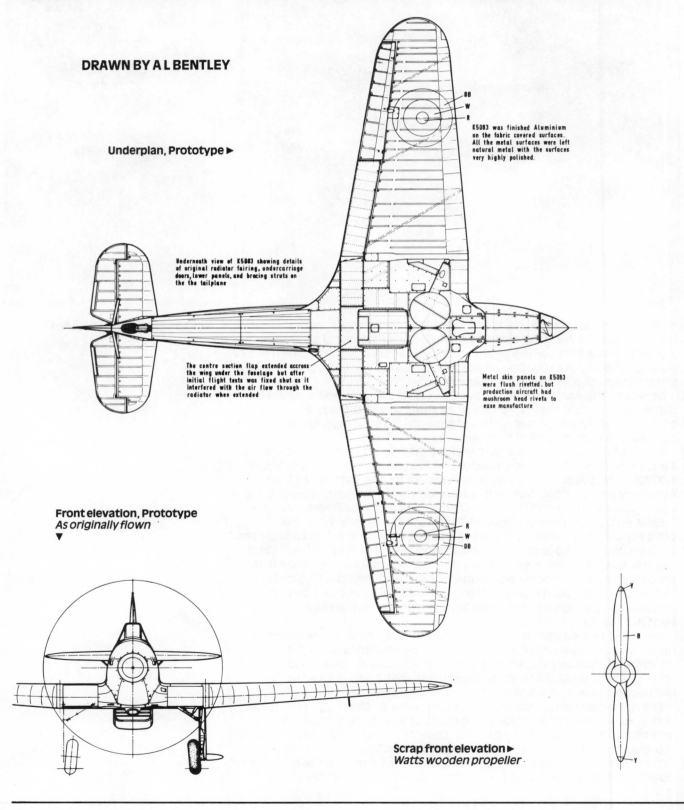

DRAWN BY A L BENTLEY

Underplan, Prototype ▶

K5083 was finished Aluminium on the fabric covered surfaces. All the metal surfaces were left natural metal with the surfaces very highly polished.

Underneath view of K5083 showing details of original radiator fairing, undercarriage doors, lower panels, and bracing struts on the the tailplane

The centre section flap extended accross the wing under the fuselage but after initial flight tests was fixed shut as it interfered with the air flow through the radiator when extended

Metal skin panels on K5083 were flush rivetted. but production aircraft had mushroom head rivets to ease manufacture

Front elevation, Prototype
As originally flown
▼

Scrap front elevation ▶
Watts wooden propeller

4

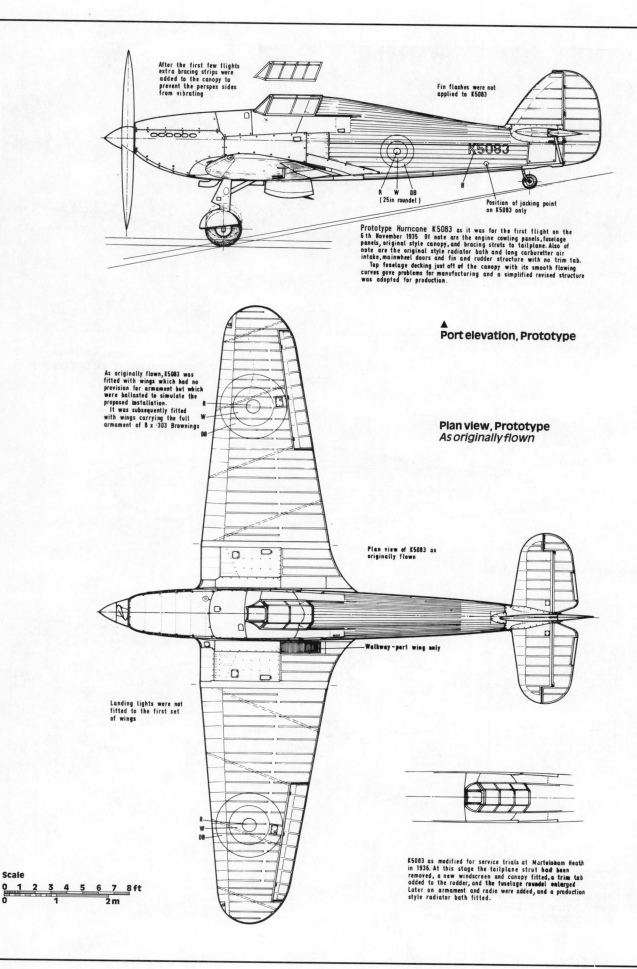

After the first few flights extra bracing strips were added to the canopy to prevent the perspex sides from vibrating

Fin flashes were not applied to K5083

K5083

R W DB
(25in roundel)

Position of jacking point on K5083 only

Prototype Hurricane K5083 as it was for the first flight on the 6th November 1935 Of note are the engine cowling panels, fuselage panels, original style canopy, and bracing struts to tailplane. Also of note are the original style radiator bath and long carburetter air intake, mainwheel doors and fin and rudder structure with no trim tab.
Top fuselage decking just aft of the canopy with its smooth flowing curves gave problems for manufacturing and a simplified revised structure was adopted for production.

▲
Port elevation, Prototype

Plan view, Prototype
As originally flown

As originally flown, K5083 was fitted with wings which had no provision for armament but which were ballasted to simulate the proposed installation.
It was subsequently fitted with wings carrying the full armament of 8 x ·303 Brownings

R
W
DB

Plan view of K5083 as originally flown

Walkway-port wing only

Landing lights were not fitted to the first set of wings

R
W
DB

K5083 as modified for service trials at Martlesham Heath in 1936. At this stage the tailplane strut had been removed, a new windscreen and canopy fitted, a trim tab added to the rudder, and the fuselage roundel enlarged Later on armament and radio were added, and a production style radiator bath fitted.

Scale

0 1 2 3 4 5 6 7 8 ft

0   1   2m

▲ **Brooklands-built, metal-winged Hurricane Mk I photographed prewar. Port wing has black undersurfaces – compare leading-edge colour boundaries.**

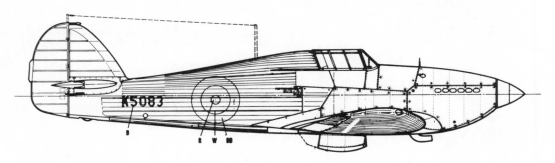

Starboard elevation, Prototype ▲

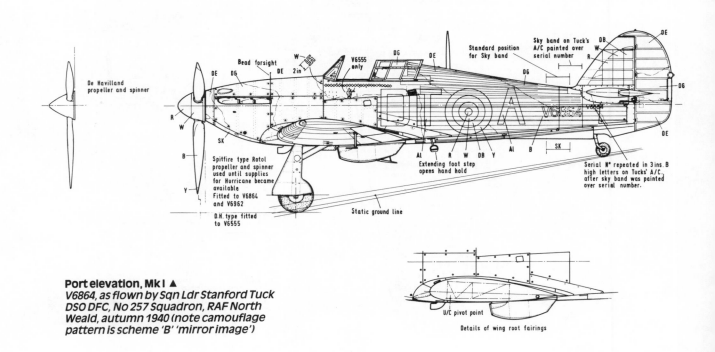

De Havilland propeller and spinner

Spitfire type Rotol propeller and spinner used until supplies for Hurricane became available
Fitted to V6864 and V6962

D.H. type fitted to V6555

Bead forsight

V6555 only

Standard position for Sky band

Sky band on Tuck's A/C painted over serial number

Extending foot step opens hand hold

Static ground line

Serial N° repeated in 3 ins. B high letters on Tucks' A/C. after sky band was painted over serial number.

Port elevation, Mk I ▲
V6864, as flown by Sqn Ldr Stanford Tuck DSO DFC, No 257 Squadron, RAF North Weald, autumn 1940 (note camouflage pattern is scheme 'B' 'mirror image')

U/C pivot point

Details of wing root fairings

Side view of an early production aircraft showing the revised fuselage
lines aft of the canopy, retractable tailwheel (fixed down after a few
months in service), original production style windscreen and canopy,
early radio mast, initial production standard exhausts, and
instrumentation venturi.

Early type of
external armour

DG   DE

DG   DE

Serial Nº B

DG

DG

DE

K   W   DG   Y

Undersurfaces Al

▲ Port elevation, Mk I
Early production aircraft

Scale

0 1 2 3 4 5 6 7 8 ft
0   1   2 m

Exhaust glare shields were
fitted to many Hurricanes to
improve night flying capabilities

DE   MS

DE

MS

DE   B

DG   DE

W

R

MS

P2627

B

Vokes air filter

R   W   DG   Y

Undersurfaces AB

Port elevation, Mk I ▶
P2627, No 274 Squadron

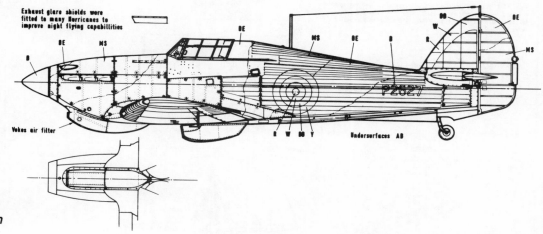

DSG

DSG

DG   DSG

DSG   EDSG

EDSG   DSG   B   R

DSG   EDSG

B

V6741

Undersurfaces Sk

R   W   DG   Y

Catapult pick up point
Sea Hurricane Mk.IA

Sea Hurricane Mk IA.   8 x ·303 Machine guns, No hook-catapult fittings only.
Sea Hurricane Mk IB.   8 x ·303 Machine guns, Arrester hook.
Sea Hurricane Mk IC.   4 x 20mm Cannons.   Arrester hook.

Details of the lower rear fuselage panels
of the Sea Hurricane Mk's IB & IC

▲ **Port elevation, Sea Hurricane Mk IC**

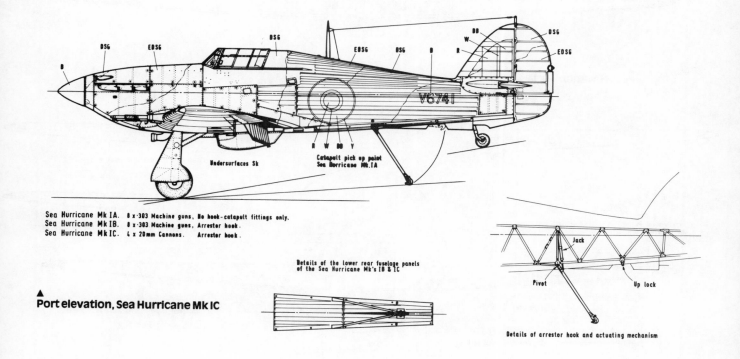

Jack

Pivot

Up lock

Details of arrestor hook and actuating mechanism

7

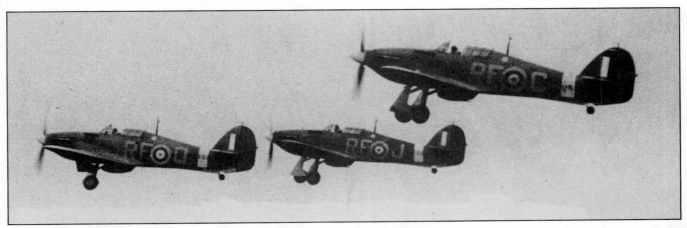

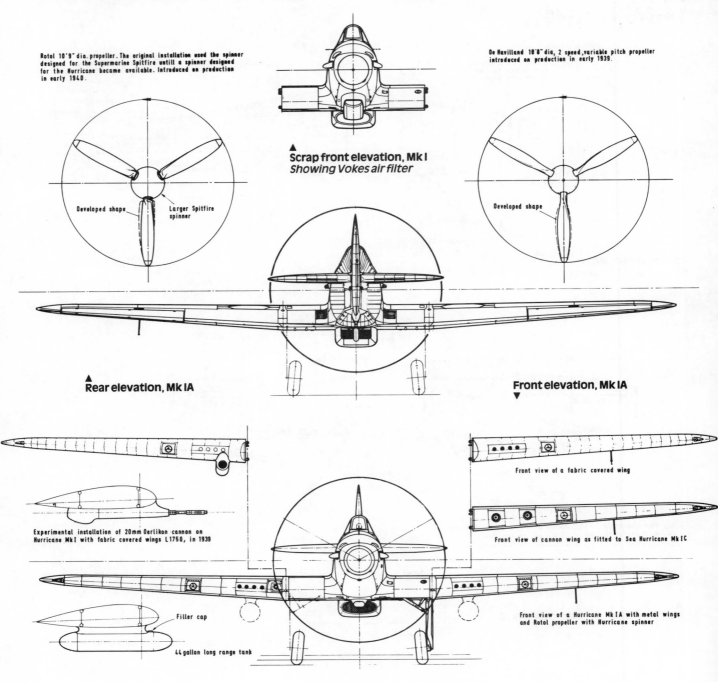

Rotol 10'9" dia. propeller. The original installation used the spinner designed for the Supermarine Spitfire untill a spinner designed for the Hurricane became available. Introduced on production in early 1940.

De Havilland 10'8" dia, 2 speed, variable pitch propeller introduced on production in early 1939.

▲ **Scrap front elevation, Mk I**
Showing Vokes air filter

Developed shape   Larger Spitfire spinner

Developed shape

▲ **Rear elevation, Mk IA**

Front elevation, Mk IA ▼

Experimental installation of 20mm Oerlikon cannon on Hurricane Mk I with fabric covered wings L1750, in 1939

Front view of a fabric covered wing

Front view of cannon wing as fitted to Sea Hurricane Mk IC

Filler cap

44 gallon long range tank

Front view of a Hurricane Mk IA with metal wings and Rotol propeller with Hurricane spinner

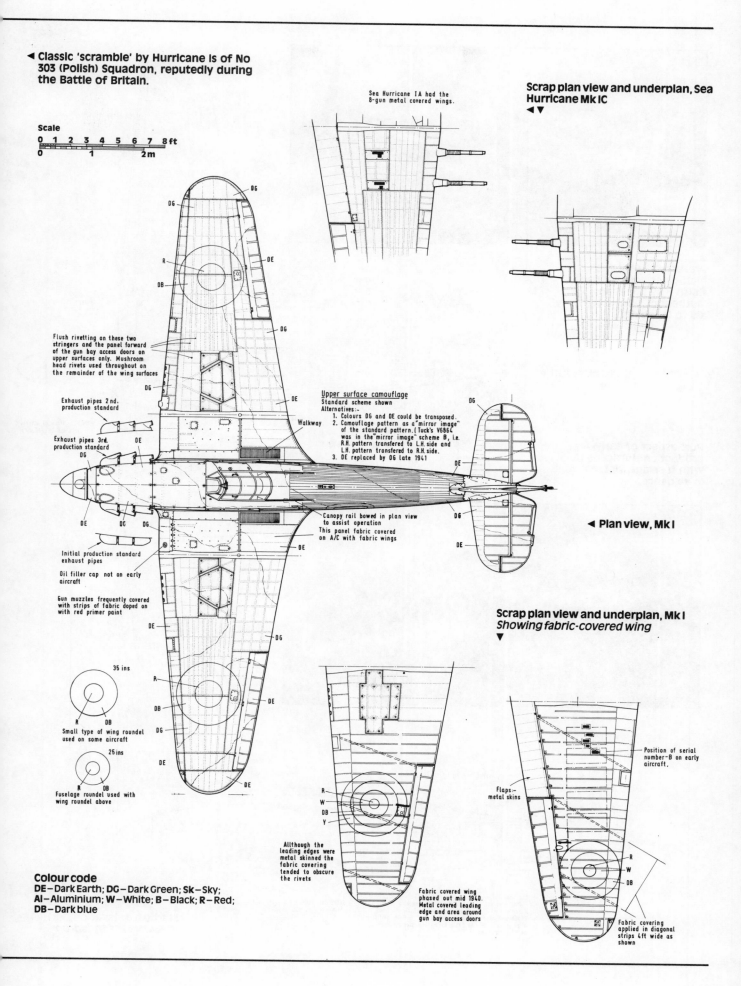

◄ Classic 'scramble' by Hurricane is of No 303 (Polish) Squadron, reputedly during the Battle of Britain.

Scale

0 1 2 3 4 5 6 7 8 ft
0 1 2 m

Sea Hurricane IA had the 8-gun metal covered wings.

Scrap plan view and underplan, Sea Hurricane Mk IC
◄ ▼

Flush rivetting on these two stringers and the panel forward of the gun bay access doors on upper surfaces only. Mushroom head rivets used throughout on the remainder of the wing surfaces

Exhaust pipes 2nd. production standard

Exhaust pipes 3rd. production standard

Initial production standard exhaust pipes

Oil filler cap not on early aircraft

Gun muzzles frequently covered with strips of fabric doped on with red primer paint

Upper surface camouflage
Standard scheme shown
Alternatives:-
1. Colours DG and DE could be transposed.
2. Camouflage pattern as a "mirror image" of the standard pattern. (Tuck's V6864 was in the "mirror image" scheme B, i.e. R.H. pattern transferred to L.H. side and L.H. pattern transferred to R.H. side.
3. DE replaced by DG late 1941

Walkway

Canopy rail bowed in plan view to assist operation
This panel fabric covered on A/C with fabric wings

◄ Plan view, Mk I

35 ins

Small type of wing roundel used on some aircraft

25 ins

Fuselage roundel used with wing roundel above

Scrap plan view and underplan, Mk I
Showing fabric-covered wing
▼

Allthough the leading edges were metal skinned the fabric covering tended to obscure the rivets

Fabric covered wing phased out mid 1940. Metal covered leading edge and area around gun bay access doors

Position of serial number-B on early aircraft.

Flaps:- metal skins

Fabric covering applied in diagonal strips 4ft wide as shown

Colour code
DE–Dark Earth; **DG**–Dark Green; **Sk**–Sky;
Al–Aluminium; **W**–White; **B**–Black; **R**–Red;
DB–Dark blue

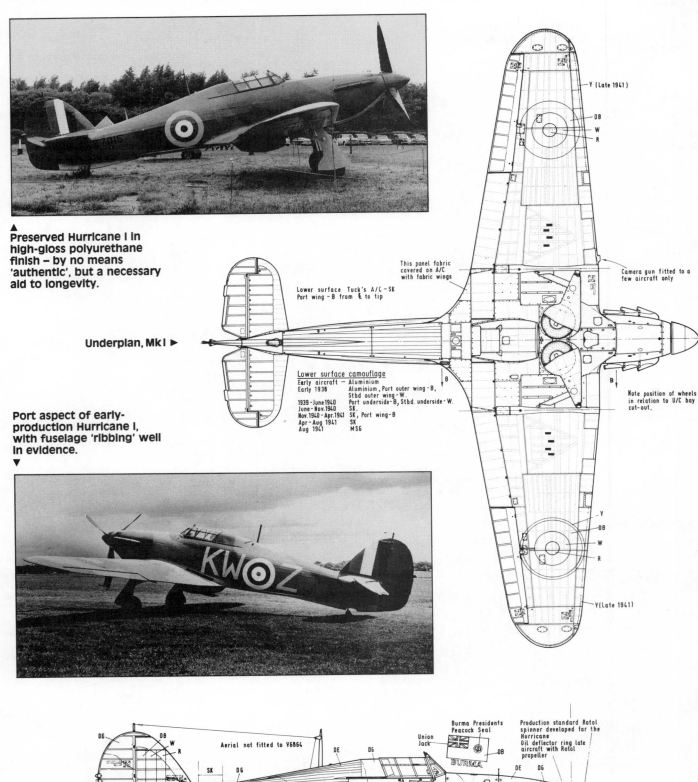

▲ **Preserved Hurricane I in high-gloss polyurethane finish – by no means 'authentic', but a necessary aid to longevity.**

Underplan, Mk I ▶

Port aspect of early-production Hurricane I, with fuselage 'ribbing' well in evidence.
▼

Y (Late 1941)

DB
W
R

This panel fabric covered on A/C with fabric wings

Camera gun fitted to a few aircraft only

Lower surface Tuck's A/C – SK
Port wing – B from ℄ to tip

Lower surface camouflage
Early aircraft — Aluminium
Early 1938   Aluminium, Port outer wing - B, Stbd outer wing - W.
1939 - June 1940   Port underside-B, Stbd. underside- W.
June - Nov. 1940   SK.
Nov. 1940 - Apr. 1941   SK, Port wing-B
Apr - Aug 1941   SK
Aug 1941   MSG

Note position of wheels in relation to U/C bay cut-out.

Y
DB
W
R

Y (Late 1941)

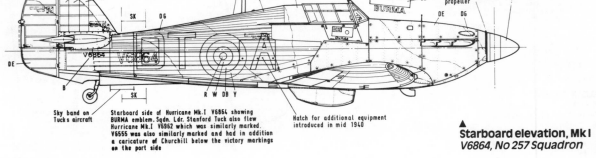

DG
DB
W
R

Aerial not fitted to V6864

SK   DG

DE

B

V6864   V6864

R W DB Y

Sky band on Tuck's aircraft

SK

DE   DG

DE   DG

Burma Presidents Peacock Seal

Union Jack

BURMA   DB

Production standard Rotol spinner developed for the Hurricane
Oil deflector ring late aircraft with Rotol propeller

DE   DG

Starboard side of Hurricane Mk.I V6864 showing BURMA emblem. Sqdn. Ldr. Stanford Tuck also flew Hurricane Mk.I V6962 which was similarly marked. V6555 was also similarly marked and had in addition a caricature of Churchill below the victory markings on the port side

Hatch for additional equipment introduced in mid 1940

▲ **Starboard elevation, Mk I**
V6864, No 257 Squadron

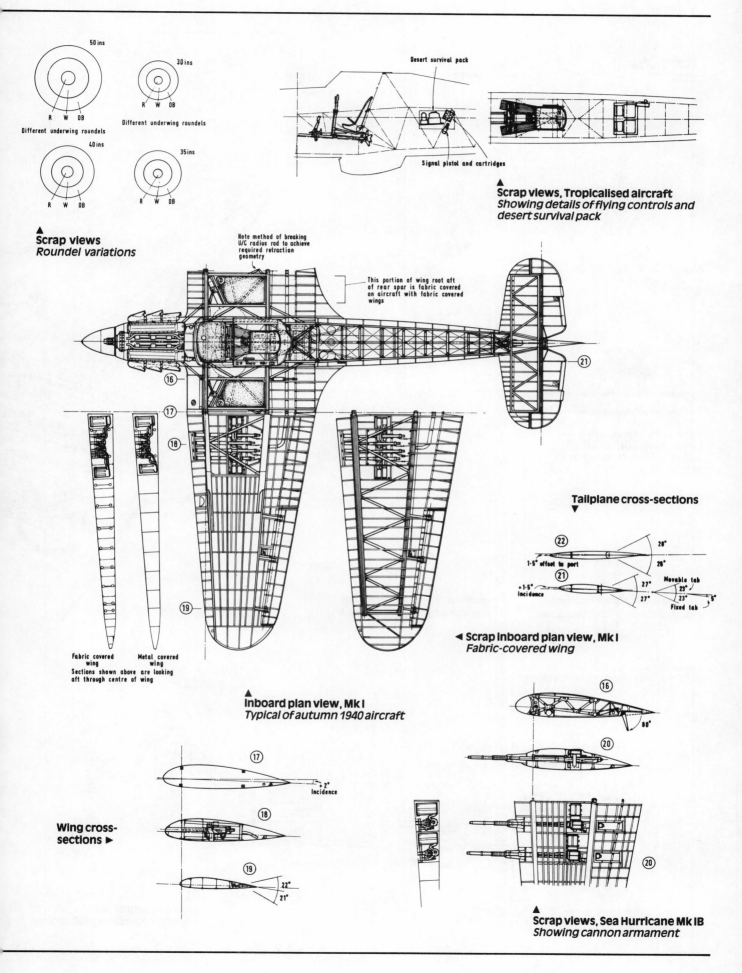

50 ins

R W DB
Different underwing roundels

30 ins

R W DB
Different underwing roundels

40 ins

R W DB

35 ins

R W DB

▲ **Scrap views**
Roundel variations

Desert survival pack

Signal pistol and cartridges

▲ **Scrap views, Tropicalised aircraft**
Showing details of flying controls and desert survival pack

Note method of breaking
U/C radius rod to achieve
required retraction
geometry

This portion of wing root aft
of rear spar is fabric covered
on aircraft with fabric covered
wings

Fabric covered
wing

Metal covered
wing

Sections shown above are looking
aft through centre of wing

▲ **Inboard plan view, Mk I**
Typical of autumn 1940 aircraft

Tailplane cross-sections
▼

1·5° offset to port

28°

28°

+1·5°
incidence

27°

27°

Movable tab

23°

23°

Fixed tab

◄ **Scrap inboard plan view, Mk I**
Fabric-covered wing

Wing cross-sections ►

2°
Incidence

22°
21°

80°

Scrap views, Sea Hurricane Mk IB
Showing cannon armament

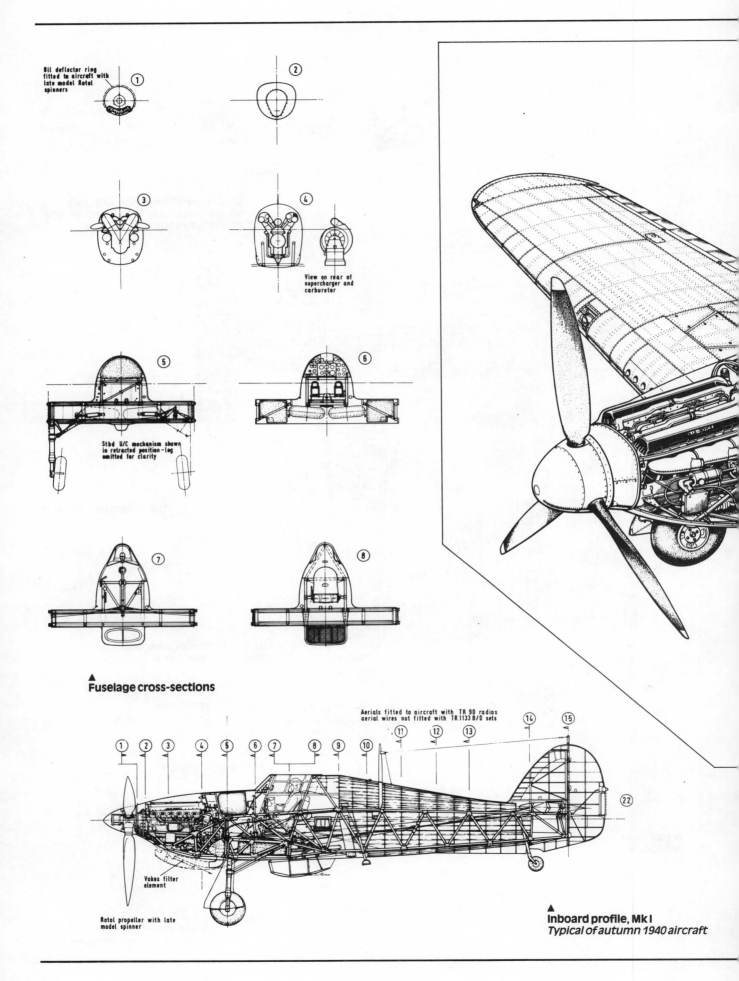

Oil deflector ring fitted to aircraft with late model Rotol spinners

① ② ③ ④

View on rear of supercharger and carburetor

⑤ ⑥

Stbd U/C mechanism shown in retracted position - leg omitted for clarity

⑦ ⑧

▲
Fuselage cross-sections

Aerials fitted to aircraft with TR 90 radios aerial wires not fitted with TR.1133 B/D sets

① ② ③ ④ ⑤ ⑥ ⑦ ⑧ ⑨ ⑩ ⑪ ⑫ ⑬ ⑭ ⑮

㉒

Vokes filter element

Rotol propeller with late model spinner

▲
Inboard profile, Mk I
Typical of autumn 1940 aircraft

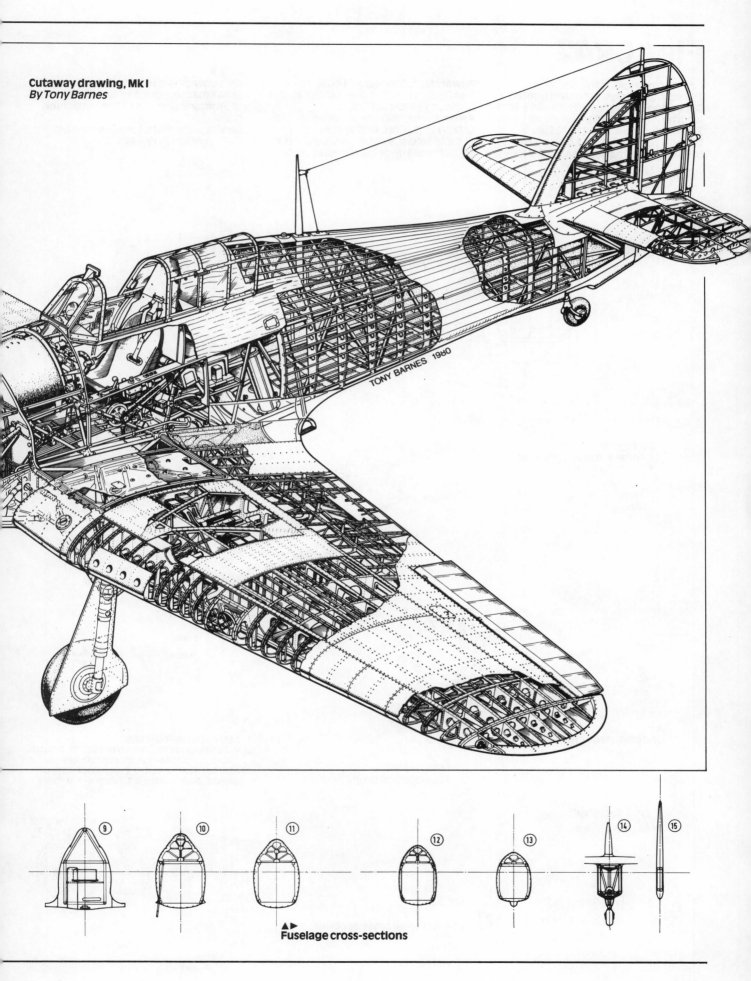

Cutaway drawing, Mk I
By Tony Barnes

TONY BARNES 1980

⑨ ⑩ ⑪ ⑫ ⑬ ⑭ ⑮

▲► **Fuselage cross-sections**

Fiat CR42

Country of origin: Italy.
Type: Single-seat, land-based fighter.
Dimensions: Wing span 31ft 9¾in *9.70m*; length 27ft 2¾in *8.30m*; height 10ft 10in *3.30m*; wing area 241 sq ft *22.39m²*.
Weights: Empty 3763lb *1707kg*; loaded 5052lb *2288kg*; maximum 5302lb *2406kg*.

Powerplant: One Fiat A74 RC38 fourteen-cylinder radial engine rated at 840hp at 12,470ft *3800m*.
Performance: Maximum speed 268mph *432kph* at 12,470ft *3800m*; time to 13,120ft *4000m*, 5.4min; service ceiling 31,000ft *9450m*; range 460 miles *740km*.

Armament: Two fixed 12.7mm Breda-SAFAT machine guns, or one fixed 12.7mm and one fixed 7.7mm machine guns.
Service: First flight (prototype) early 1939; service entry late 1939.

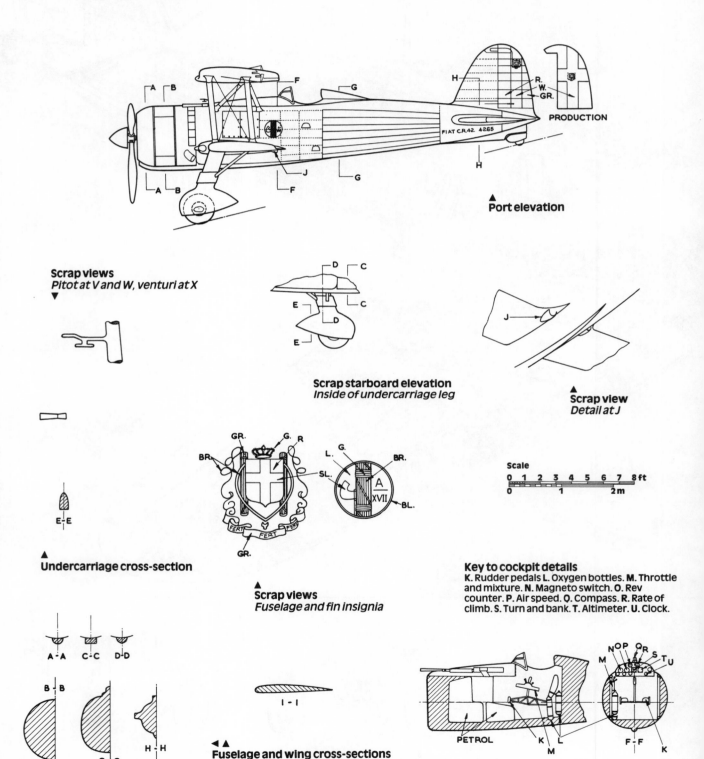

▲ Port elevation

PRODUCTION

Scrap views
Pitot at V and W, venturi at X
▼

Scrap starboard elevation
Inside of undercarriage leg

▲ Scrap view
Detail at J

▲ Undercarriage cross-section

Scale

▲ Scrap views
Fuselage and fin insignia

Key to cockpit details
K. Rudder pedals L. Oxygen bottles. M. Throttle and mixture. N. Magneto switch. O. Rev counter. P. Air speed. Q. Compass. R. Rate of climb. S. Turn and bank. T. Altimeter. U. Clock.

◄ ▲ Fuselage and wing cross-sections

PETROL

The CR42 Falco was the last biplane fighter type to be produced by any of the major powers and enjoyed only limited success.

DRAWN BY G A G COX

RIB SPACING
LOWER WING

COLOURS
REVERSED
ON N.F.
VERSION

X

L.

BL.

Colour notes
Prototype (illustrated) – Silver overall.
Production machines camouflaged in Burnt and Raw Sienna and Hookers Green, deep and pale; undersurfaces light grey. Night fighter version – Matt black overall.

Camouflage pattern

Plan view

Colour code
L – Light grey; **GR** – Green; **R** – Red; **SL** – Silver; **BL** – Black; **BR** Brown; **G** – Gold; **W** – White.

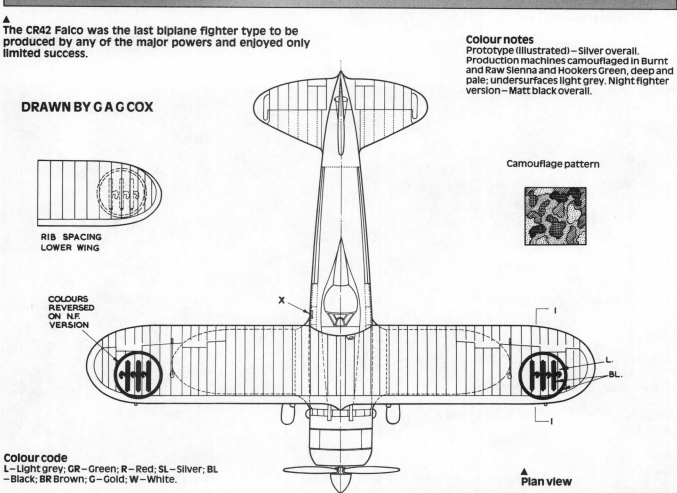

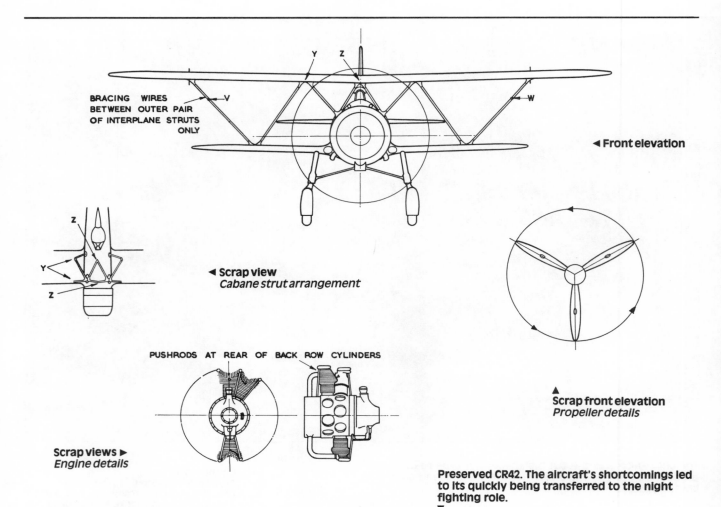

BRACING WIRES
BETWEEN OUTER PAIR
OF INTERPLANE STRUTS
ONLY

◄ **Front elevation**

◄ **Scrap view**
Cabane strut arrangement

PUSHRODS AT REAR OF BACK ROW CYLINDERS

▲
Scrap front elevation
Propeller details

Scrap views ▶
Engine details

Preserved CR42. The aircraft's shortcomings led to its quickly being transferred to the night fighting role.
▼

Fokker D23

Country of origin: The Netherlands.
Type: Prototype single-seat, land-based fighter.
Dimensions: Wing span 37ft 8¾in *11.50m*; length 35ft 1¼in *10.70m*; height 11ft *3.35m*; wing area 199.1 sq ft *18.5m²*.
Weights: Empty 5070lb *2300kg*; loaded 6612lb *3000kg*.
Powerplant: Two Walter Sagitta I-SR twelve-cylinder, air-cooled piston engines each rated at 540hp.
Performance: Maximum speed 326mph *525kph*; time to 3280ft *1000m*, 1.35min; service ceiling 29,500ft *9000m*; range 560 miles *900km*.
Armament: Two fixed 13.2mm FN-Browning machine guns and two fixed 7.9mm FN-Browning machine guns.
Service: First flight June 1939.

DRAWN BY R DAS

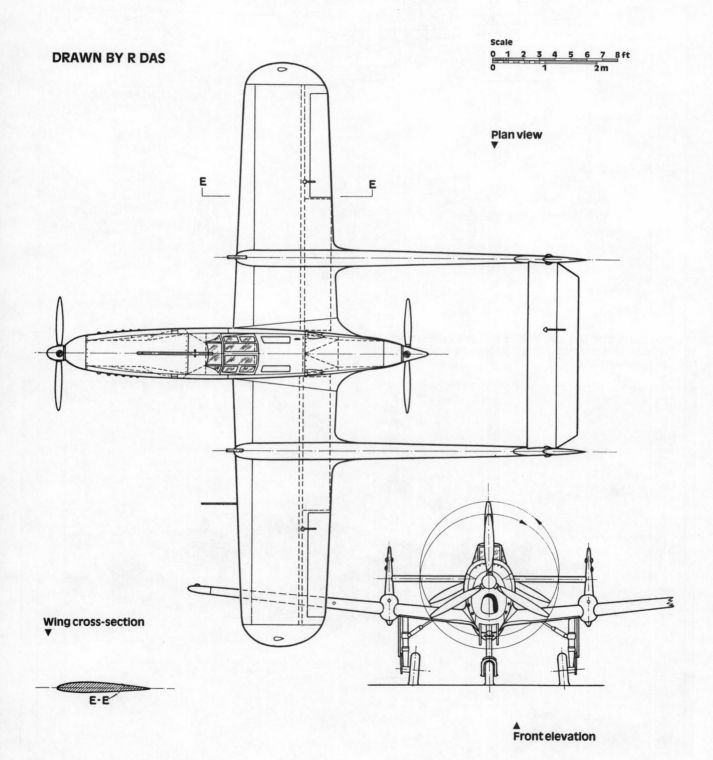

Scale
0 1 2 3 4 5 6 7 8 ft
0 1 2m

Plan view ▼

Wing cross-section ▼

E·E

Front elevation ▲

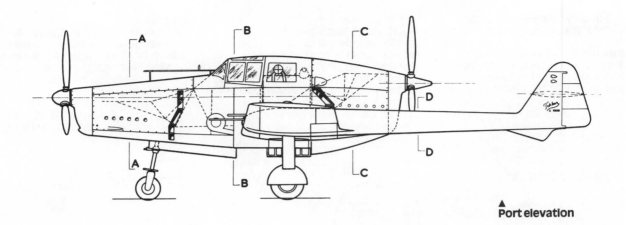

▲ Port elevation

Scale
0 1 2 3 4 5 6 7 8 ft
0 1 2 m

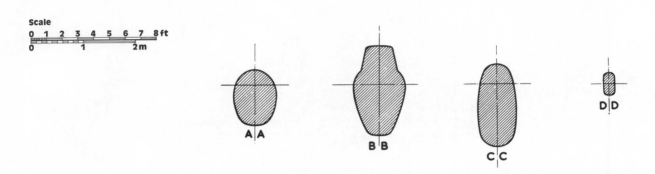

▲ Fuselage and boom cross-sections

Only one 'push-pull' D23 was built, and this was destroyed in an air raid. It was the first fighter to feature a retractable tricycle undercarriage.
▼

Messerschmitt Bf 109F-1, F-2 and F-4/Trop

Country of origin: Germany.
Type: Single-seat, land-based fighter.
Dimensions: Wing span 32ft 5¾in *9.90m*; length 29ft 0¼in *8.85m*; height 8ft 6in *2.59m*; wing area 174.38 sq ft *16.20m²*.
Weights: Empty equipped (F-2) 5188lb *2354kg*, (F-4) 5269lb *2390kg*; loaded (F-2) 6173lb *2800kg*, (F-4) 6393lb *2900kg*.
Powerplant: One Daimler-Benz DB 601N twelve-cylinder, liquid-cooled piston engine rated at 1200hp, (F-4) DB 601E-1 rated at 1350hp.
Performance: Maximum speed (F-2) 373mph *600kph* at 19,685ft *6000m*, (F-4) 388mph *625kph* at 21,325ft *6500m*; initial climb rate (F-2) 3860ft/min *1175m/min*, (F-4) 4290ft/min *1310m/min*; service ceiling (F-2) 36,100ft *11,000m*, (F-4) 39,370ft *12,000m*; range about 450 miles *725km*.
Armament: Two fixed 7.9mm MG 17 machine guns, plus (F-2) one fixed 15mm MG 151 cannon or (F-4) one fixed 20mm MG 151 cannon.
Service: First flight (Bf 109V-1) September 1935, (modified Bf 109E) 10 July 1940; service entry (F-1) January 1941.

DRAWN BY A A P LLOYD AND J D CARRICK

Port elevation, Bf 109F-4/Trop
▼

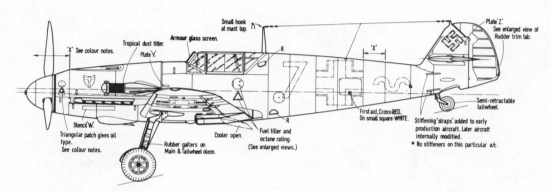

'X' See colour notes.
Tropical dust filter.
Plate 'Y.'
Armour glass screen.
Small hook at mast top.
Plate 'Z.'
See enlarged view of Rudder trim tab.
'X'
R
R
Stencil 'W.'
Triangular patch gives oil type.
See colour notes.
Rubber gaiters on Main & Tailwheel oleos.
Cooler open.
Fuel filler and octane rating.
(See enlarged views.)
First aid, Cross-RED. On small square-WHITE.
Semi-retractable tailwheel.
Stiffening 'straps' added to early production aircraft. Later aircraft internally modified.
* No stiffeners on this particular a/c.

Scale
0 1 2 3 4 5 6 7 8 ft
0   1   2m

Bf 109Fs under production, with swastikas on tails half-heartedly scratched out on the negative. Octane triangles are prominent behind cockpit.
▼

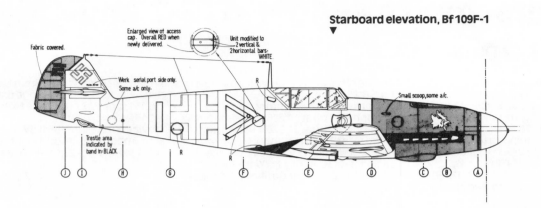

Starboard elevation, Bf 109F-1
▼

Enlarged view of access cap. Overall RED when newly delivered.

Unit modified to 2 vertical & 2 horizontal bars: WHITE.

Fabric covered.

Werk serial port side only. Some a/c only.

Small scoop, some a/c.

Trestle area indicated by band in BLACK.

Ⓙ Ⓘ Ⓗ Ⓖ R R Ⓕ Ⓔ Ⓓ Ⓒ Ⓑ Ⓐ

Scrap views
External markings details (enlarged)
▼

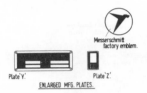

Messerschmitt factory emblem.

87
C-3

Enlarged octane rating triangles. (Either C-3 or 87.)
See colour notes.

Plate 'Y'. Plate 'Z'.

ENLARGED MFG. PLATES.

Vorsicht beim Öffnen
Kühler ist im Haubenteil eingebaut

ENGINE COWLING, STENCIL 'W'.

J.G. 27.
BLACK: Cross.
WHITE: Shield.
YELLOW: Aircraft & Border.

J.G. 2. .
BLACK: Head.
RED: Comb, Tongue & Wattle.
YELLOW: Beak.
WHITE: Eye & Highlights

J.G. 2. 'Richthofen'
RED: Script 'R'.
WHITE: Shield.
BLACK: Border.

Colour notes, BF109F-4/Trop
Drawings show North African colours of III/JG27, Libya, 1942. Uppersurfaces – Sand yellow (light brown); undersurfaces – pale blue. Areas 'X' – white (spinner, nose panels back to 'X', rear fuselage band). Number '7' and symbol aft of cross – white outlined thinly black. Werk nr unknown. Wing tips – white.

Colour notes, Bf 109F-1
Drawings show III/JG2 aircraft flown by *Hauptmann* Hans 'Assi' Hahn, France, 1941. Uppersurfaces – black-green and dark green, 'soft-edged' splinter pattern; fuselage – dark green mottle over undersurface colour; undersurfaces – pale blue. Entire engine cowling and rudder – yellow. Bar and chevron – white thinly outlined black. Wing root and exhaust panels – black. Spinner – white. Thirty-one 'kill' bars and serial 'W Nr 5749' – black. **Note:** This machine did not have the extra armour glass windscreen (normally standard only on F-4 sub-types onward).

Three-quarter front view of Bf 109V24 prototype highlights bulbous spinner of the F variant and delicate splayed undercarriage, though this machine retains the cropped wing tips of the E from which it was converted.
▼

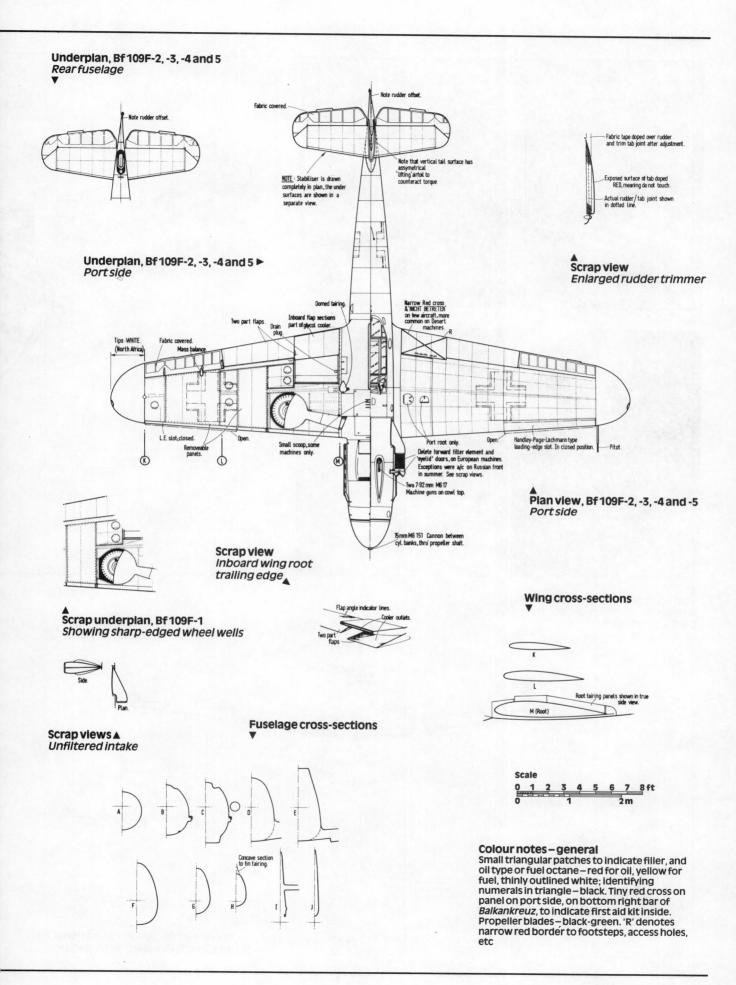

Underplan, Bf 109F-2, -3, -4 and 5
Rear fuselage
▼

Note rudder offset.

Note rudder offset.

Fabric covered.

NOTE : Stabiliser is drawn completely in plan, the under surfaces are shown in a separate view.

Note that vertical tail surface has assymetrical 'lifting' airfoil to counteract torque.

Underplan, Bf 109F-2, -3, -4 and 5 ►
Port side

Scrap view
Enlarged rudder trimmer
▲

Fabric tape doped over rudder and trim tab joint after adjustment.

Exposed surface of tab doped RED, meaning do not touch.

Actual rudder / tab joint shown in dotted line.

Domed fairing.

Inboard flap sections part of glycol cooler.

Two part flaps.

Drain plug.

Narrow Red cross & 'NICHT BETRETEN' on few aircraft, more common on Desert machines.

Tips : WHITE. (North Africa)

Fabric covered.

Mass balance.

L.E. slot; closed.

Removeable panels.

Open.

Small scoop, some machines only.

Port root only.

Delete forward filter element and 'eyelid' doors, on European machines. Exceptions were a/c on Russian front in summer. See scrap views.

Two 7.92 mm MG 17 Machine guns on cowl top.

15 mm MG 151 Cannon between cyl. banks, thru' propeller shaft.

Open.

Handley-Page-Lachmann type leading-edge slot. In closed position.

Pitot.

Plan view, Bf 109F-2, -3, -4 and -5
Port side
▲

Scrap view
Inboard wing root trailing edge ▲

Scrap underplan, Bf 109F-1
Showing sharp-edged wheel wells
▲

Side.

Plan.

Flap angle indicator lines.

Cooler outlets.

Two part flaps

Wing cross-sections
▼

K

L

Root fairing panels shown in true side view.

M (Root)

Scrap views ▲
Unfiltered intake

Fuselage cross-sections
▼

A   B   C   D   E

Concave section to fin fairing.

F   G   H   I   J

Scale

0 1 2 3 4 5 6 7 8 ft
0   1   2 m

Colour notes – general
Small triangular patches to indicate filler, and oil type or fuel octane – red for oil, yellow for fuel, thinly outlined white; identifying numerals in triangle – black. Tiny red cross on panel on port side, on bottom right bar of *Balkankreuz*, to indicate first aid kit inside. Propeller blades – black-green. 'R' denotes narrow red border to footsteps, access holes, etc

▲
Two photos depicting the cockpit interior. Gun sight is absent from this particular aircraft.

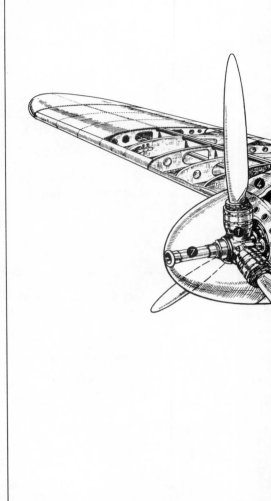

Front elevation, Bf 109F-4/Trop
▼

Sideways hinged canopy.

Oil cooler.
(Engine lubricant.)

Glycol cooler.
(Engine coolant.)

✷ See notes.

Scrap view
Detail of cowl fastener
▼

DETAIL OF COWL
FASTENER

'Dzus' type
fastener with RED
bars to denote
locked position.

Letters 'Zu' not
common.

Scrap side view of
cooler, gill & flap open.

▲
Scrap view
Cooler, gill and flap open

Scale

0 1 2 3 4 5 6 7 8 ft

0   1   2 m

Preserved Bf 109F at the National Air and Space Museum in the USA. ▶

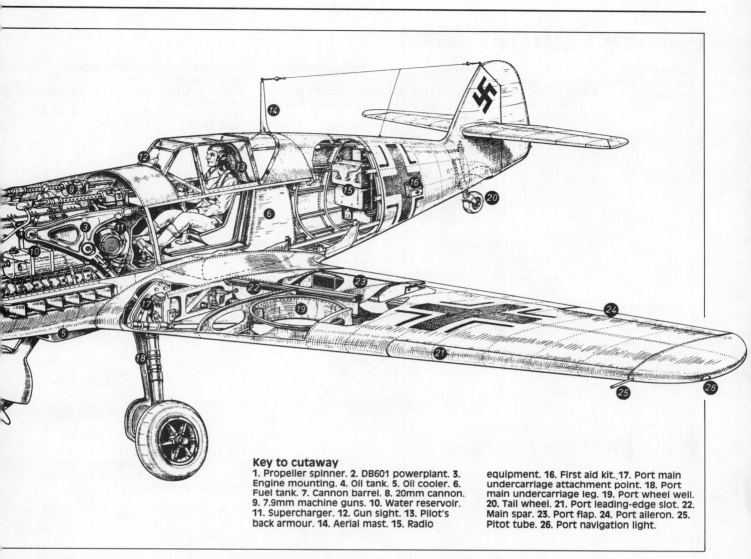

Key to cutaway

1. Propeller spinner. 2. DB601 powerplant. 3. Engine mounting. 4. Oil tank. 5. Oil cooler. 6. Fuel tank. 7. Cannon barrel. 8. 20mm cannon. 9. 7.9mm machine guns. 10. Water reservoir. 11. Supercharger. 12. Gun sight. 13. Pilot's back armour. 14. Aerial mast. 15. Radio equipment. 16. First aid kit. 17. Port main undercarriage attachment point. 18. Port main undercarriage leg. 19. Port wheel well. 20. Tail wheel. 21. Port leading-edge slot. 22. Main spar. 23. Port flap. 24. Port aileron. 25. Pitot tube. 26. Port navigation light.

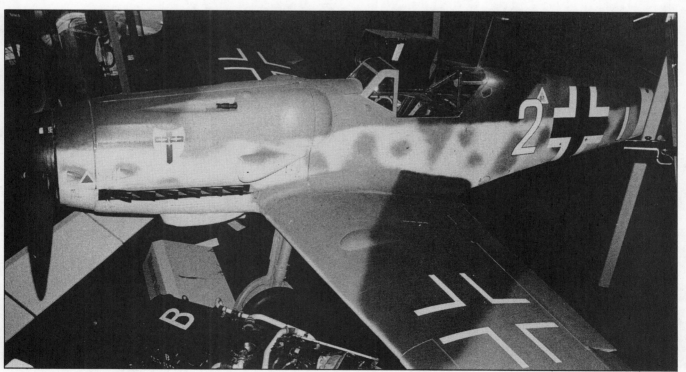

Fairey Fulmar Mk I

Country of origin: Great Britain.
Type: Two-seat, carrier-based fighter.
Dimensions: Wing span 46ft 4½in *14.14m*; length 40ft 2in *12.24m*; height 10ft 8in *3.25m*; wing area 342 sq ft *31.76m²*.
Weights: Empty 7385lb *3350kg*; normal

loaded about 9600lb *4350kg*; maximum about 10,000lb *4540kg*.
Powerplant: One Rolls-Royce Merlin VIII V12, liquid-cooled piston engine rated at 1145hp.
Performance: Maximum speed 272mph *438kph*; initial climb rate 1320ft/min

402m/min; service ceiling 27,200ft *8290m*; range 780 miles *1255km*.
Armament: Eight fixed 0.303in Browning machine guns.
Service: First flight (prototype) 4 January 1940; service entry July 1940.

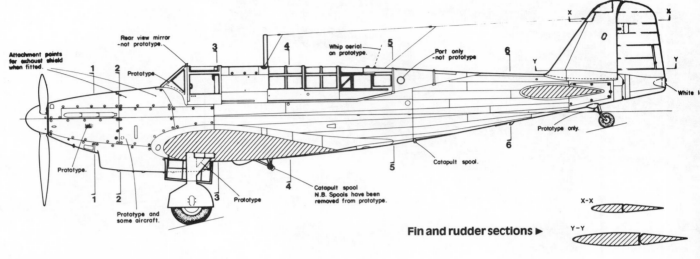

▲ **Port elevation**

Fin and rudder sections ▶

A Fulmar about to catch the wires. Note the broad-track main undercarriage and the protective covers over the gun muzzles along the wing leading edges.
▼

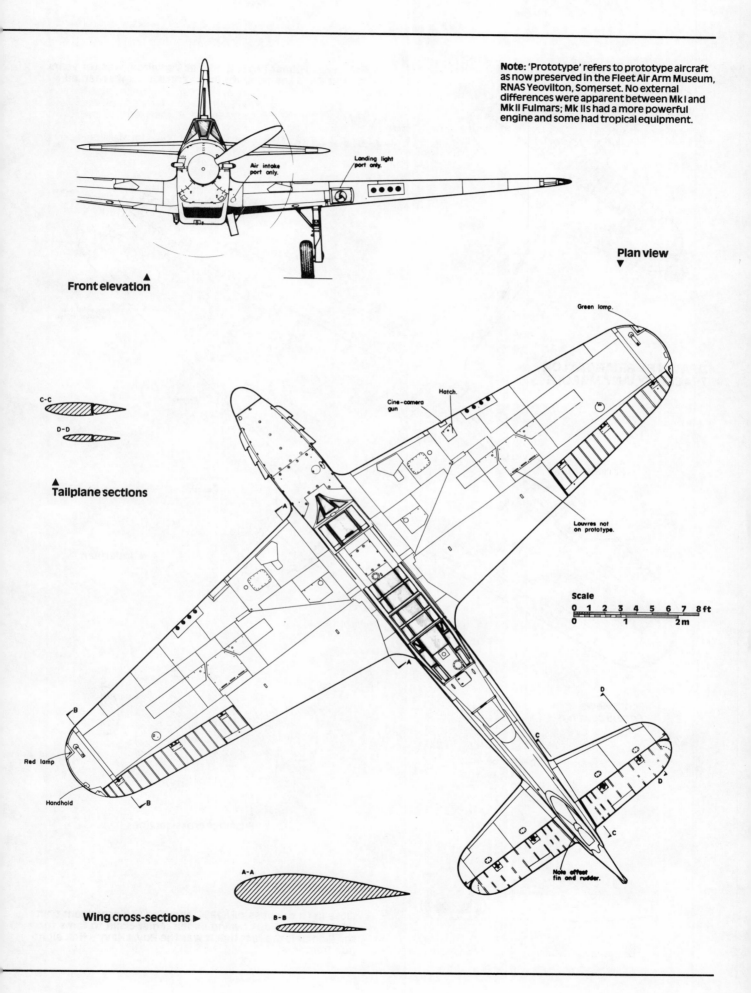

Front elevation ▲

Air intake
port only.

Landing light
port only.

Plan view
▼

Note: 'Prototype' refers to prototype aircraft
as now preserved in the Fleet Air Arm Museum,
RNAS Yeovilton, Somerset. No external
differences were apparent between Mk I and
Mk II Fulmars; Mk IIs had a more powerful
engine and some had tropical equipment.

Green lamp.

C-C

D-D

Tailplane sections ▲

Cine-camera
gun

Hatch.

Louvres not
on prototype.

Scale

0 1 2 3 4 5 6 7 8 ft

0   1   2 m

B

Red lamp

Handhold

B

D

C

D

Note offset
fin and rudder.

C

A-A

Wing cross-sections ►

B-B

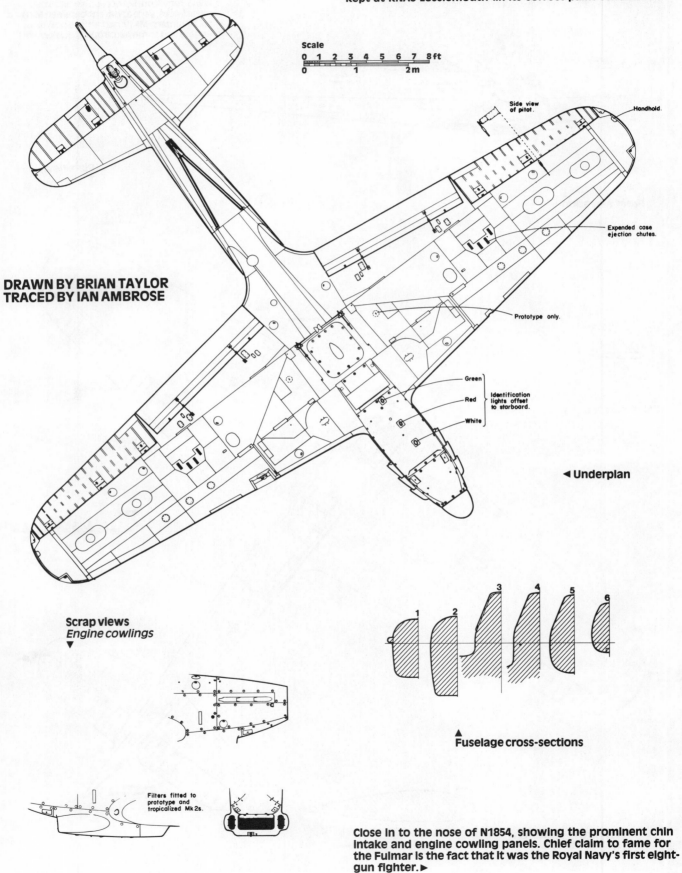

Preserved Fulmar I N1854, now at Yeovilton, was for years kept at RNAS Losslemouth (in its correct paint scheme!). ▶

Scale
0 1 2 3 4 5 6 7 8 ft
0 1 2 m

Side view of pitot.

Handhold.

Expended case ejection chutes.

Prototype only.

DRAWN BY BRIAN TAYLOR
TRACED BY IAN AMBROSE

Green
Red
White

Identification lights offset to starboard.

◀ Underplan

Scrap views
Engine cowlings
▼

3 4 5 6
1 2

▲ **Fuselage cross-sections**

Filters fitted to prototype and tropicalized Mk 2s.

Close In to the nose of N1854, showing the prominent chin Intake and engine cowling panels. Chief claim to fame for the Fulmar Is the fact that It was the Royal Navy's first eight-gun fighter. ▶

Macchi C202 Folgore

Country of origin: Italy.
Type: Single-seat, land-based fighter and fighter-bomber.
Dimensions: Wing span 34ft 8½in *10.58m*; length 29ft 1in *8.87m*; height 9ft 10in *3.00m*; wing area 180.8 sq ft *16.8m²*.
Weights: Empty 5181lb *2352kg*; normal loaded 6303lb *2860kg*; maximum 6636lb *3011kg*.

Powerplant: One Daimler-Benz DB 601A-1 (Alfa Romeo RA1000 RC41-I Monsini) twelve-cylinder, inverted-vee, liquid-cooled piston engine rated at 1200hp at 16,000ft *4875m*.
Performance: Maximum speed 330mph *531kph* at 18,050ft *5500m*; time to 3280ft

1000m, 36sec; service ceiling 34,450ft *10,500m*; range 475 miles *765km*.
Armament: Two fixed 12.7mm Breda-SAFAT and two fixed 7.7mm Breda-SAFAT machine guns.
Service: First flight (prototype) 10 August 1940; service entry November 1941.

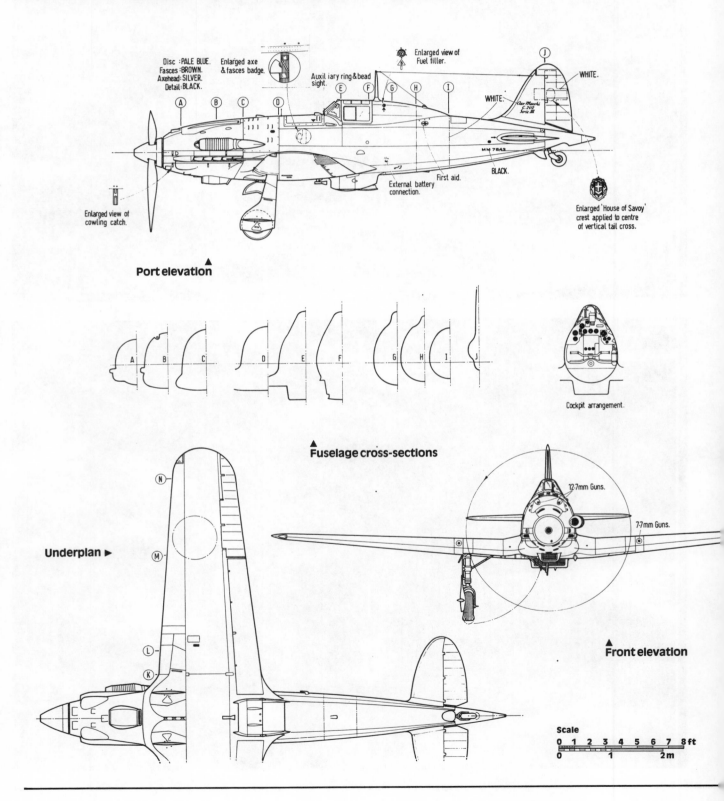

Disc : PALE BLUE.
Fasces : BROWN.
Axehead : SILVER.
Detail : BLACK.

Enlarged axe & fasces badge.

Auxiliary ring & bead sight.

Enlarged view of Fuel filler.

WHITE.

WHITE.

Clas Macchi C.202 Serie III

BLACK.

MM 7843

Enlarged view of cowling catch.

External battery connection.

First aid.

Enlarged 'House of Savoy' crest applied to centre of vertical tail cross.

▲ **Port elevation**

▲ **Fuselage cross-sections**

Cockpit arrangement.

Underplan ►

12·7mm Guns.

7·7mm Guns.

▲ **Front elevation**

Scale
0 1 2 3 4 5 6 7 8 ft
0 1 2m

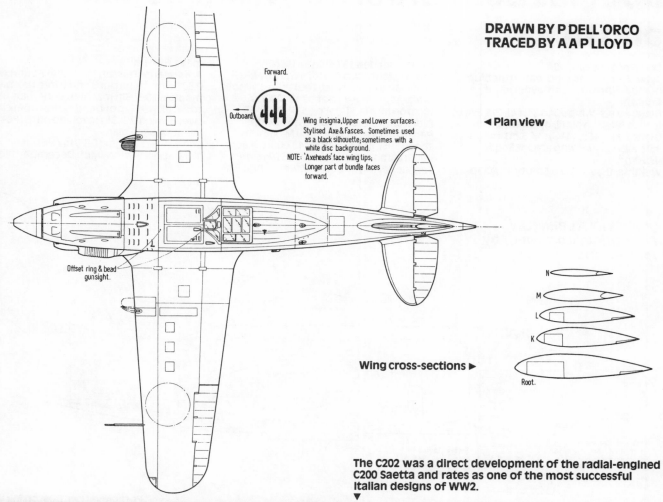

**DRAWN BY P DELL'ORCO
TRACED BY A A P LLOYD**

Forward.

Outboard.

Wing insignia, Upper and Lower surfaces. Stylised Axe & Fasces. Sometimes used as a black silhouette; sometimes with a white disc background.
NOTE: 'Axeheads' face wing tips; Longer part of bundle faces forward.

◄ **Plan view**

Offset ring & bead gunsight.

N

M

L

K

Root.

Wing cross-sections ►

The C202 was a direct development of the radial-engined C200 Saetta and rates as one of the most successful Italian designs of WW2.
▼

Douglas Boston Mks III–V, Havoc Mks I and III

Country of origin: USA.
Type: Three-seat, land-based medium bomber/intruder or (Havoc) night fighter.
Dimensions: Wing span 61ft 4in *18.69m*; length (Boston Mk III) 48ft 4in *14.73m*, (Havoc Mk I) 46ft 11¾in *14.32m*; height 15ft 10in *4.83m*; wing area 465 sq ft *43.20m²*.
Weights: (Havoc Mk I) Empty 11,400lb

5172kg; loaded 19,040lb *8639kg*.
Powerplant: Two Pratt & Whitney R-1830-S3C4G Twin Wasp fourteen-cylinder radial engines each rated at 1200hp, (Boston Mks III, IIIA) Wright R-2600-23 radial engines each rated at 1600hp.
Performance: (Havoc Mk I) Maximum speed 295mph *475kph* at 13,000ft *3960m*; initial climb rate 2000ft/min *610m/min*; service ceiling 25,300ft *7710m*; range 996

miles *1604km*.
Armament: (Boston Mk III, IIIA) Four fixed 0.303in machine guns and three flexibly mounted 0.303in machine guns, plus up to 2400lb *1089kg* of bombs, (Havoc Mk I) twelve fixed 0.303in machine guns. For variations see plans.
Service: First flight (DB-7) 17 August 1937; service entry (Mk I) December 1940.

DRAWN BY A L BENTLEY
From original drawings by John Alcorn

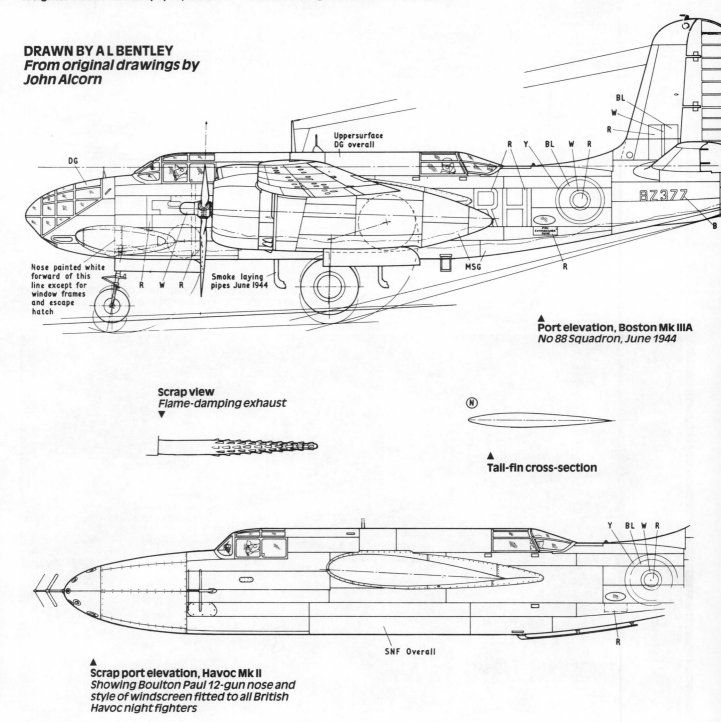

▲ **Port elevation, Boston Mk IIIA**
No 88 Squadron, June 1944

Scrap view
Flame-damping exhaust
▼

Ⓝ

▲
Tail-fin cross-section

▲
Scrap port elevation, Havoc Mk II
Showing Boulton Paul 12-gun nose and style of windscreen fitted to all British Havoc night fighters

▲ **Most Boston IIIs (DB-7Bs) were employed by the RAF as medium day bombers but some were equipped as intruders. AL399 here features gun troughs in the nose but no 'blisters'.**

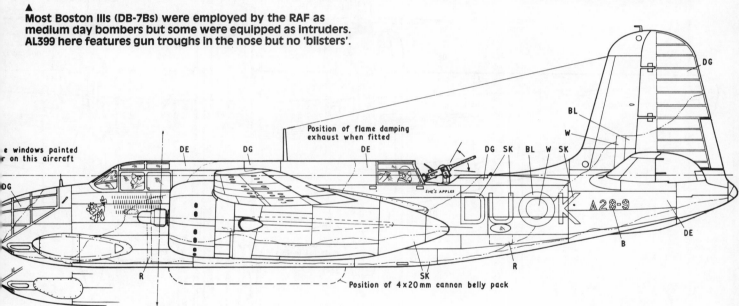

e windows painted r on this aircraft

DE DG DE

Position of flame damping exhaust when fitted

DG SK BL W SK

DG BL W

SHE'S APPLES DUOK A28-9 DG

B DE

R SK R

Position of 4×20mm cannon belly pack

▲ **Port elevation, Boston Mk III**
No 22 Squadron RAAF, New Guinea, 1943

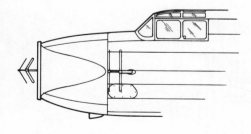

◀ **Scrap port elevation**
Turbinlite nose

Scrap port elevation ▶
Night fighter nose

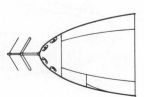

Colour code
R – Red; W – White; BL – Blue; Y – Yellow; B – Black; MB – Midnight Blue; S – Silver; DE – Dark Earth; DG – Dark Green; SK – Sky; N – Night DTD308; SNF – Special Night Finish RDM2a; OD – Olive Drab; NG – Neutral Gray; MSG – Medium Sea Grey

Scale

0 1 2 3 4 5 6 7 8ft
0 1 2m

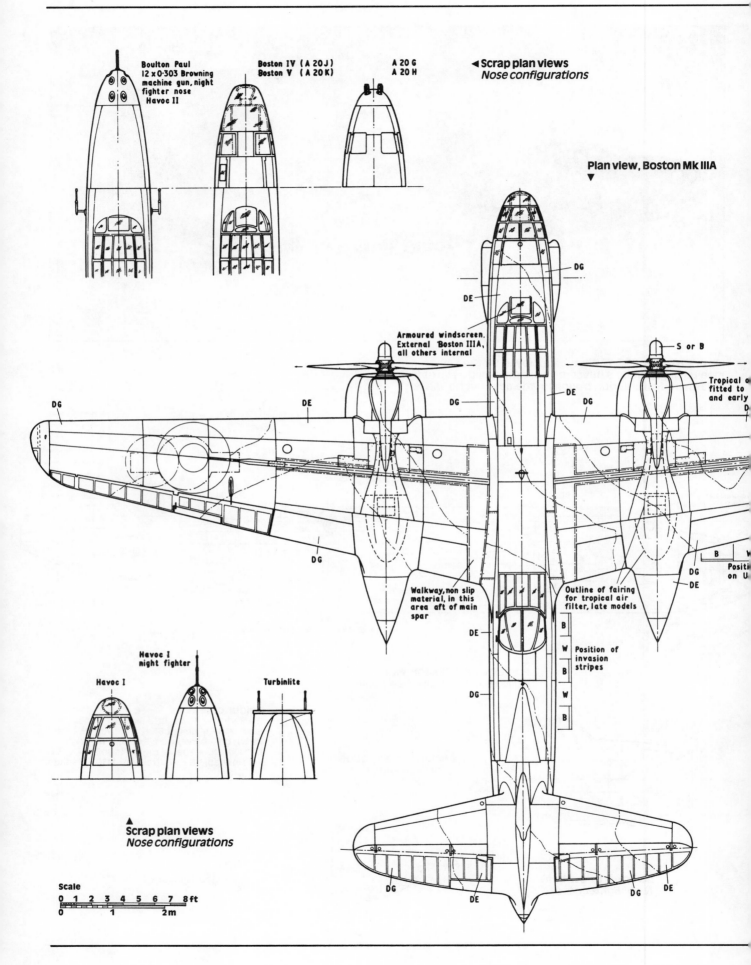

Boulton Paul
12 x 0·303 Browning
machine gun, night
fighter nose
Havoc II

Boston IV (A 20 J)
Boston V (A 20 K)

A 20 G
A 20 H

◄ **Scrap plan views**
Nose configurations

Plan view, Boston Mk IIIA
▼

DG

DE

Armoured windscreen.
External Boston IIIA,
all others internal

S or B

Tropical a
fitted to
and early

DE

DG

DG

DE

DG

DG

B   W
Positi
on U

DG

DE

Walkway, non slip
material, in this
area aft of main
spar

Outline of fairing
for tropical air
filter, late models

DE

B
W
B
W
B

Position of
invasion
stripes

DG

Havoc I
night fighter

Havoc I

Turbinlite

▲ **Scrap plan views**
Nose configurations

DG

DE

DG

DE

Scale
0 1 2 3 4 5 6 7 8 ft
0   1   2 m

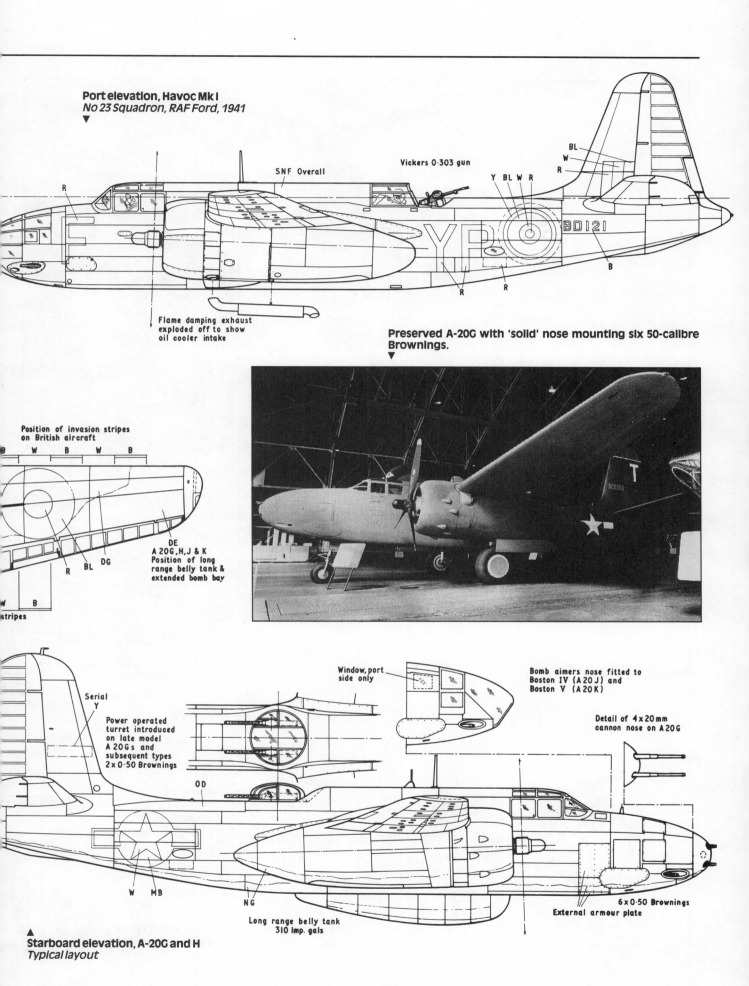

Port elevation, Havoc Mk I
No 23 Squadron, RAF Ford, 1941
▼

R

SNF Overall

Vickers 0·303 gun

Y BL W R

BL
W
R

BD121

B

R   R

YP

Flame damping exhaust
exploded off to show
oil cooler intake

Preserved A-20G with 'solid' nose mounting six 50-calibre Brownings.
▼

322208
T

Position of invasion stripes
on British aircraft

B W B W B

R BL DG

DE
A 20G,H,J & K
Position of long
range belly tank &
extended bomb bay

B

stripes

W

Serial
Y

Power operated
turret introduced
on late model
A 20Gs and
subsequent types
2 x 0·50 Brownings

OD

W MB

NG

Long range belly tank
310 Imp. gals

Window, port
side only

Bomb aimers nose fitted to
Boston IV (A20J) and
Boston V (A20K)

Detail of 4 x 20mm
cannon nose on A20G

6 x 0·50 Brownings

External armour plate

Starboard elevation, A-20G and H
Typical layout
▲

▲
US Ninth Air Force A-20G Havoc intruders en route to deliver a blow at the enemy, 1944. Note dorsal turrets.

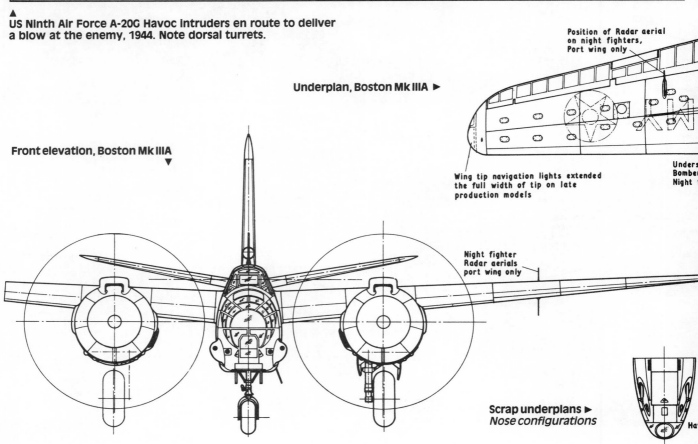

Underplan, Boston Mk IIIA ▶

Position of Radar aerial
on night fighters,
Port wing only

Wing tip navigation lights extended
the full width of tip on late
production models

Undersu
Bombers
Night fig

Front elevation, Boston Mk IIIA
▼

Night fighter
Radar aerials
port wing only

Scrap underplans ▶
Nose configurations

Havo

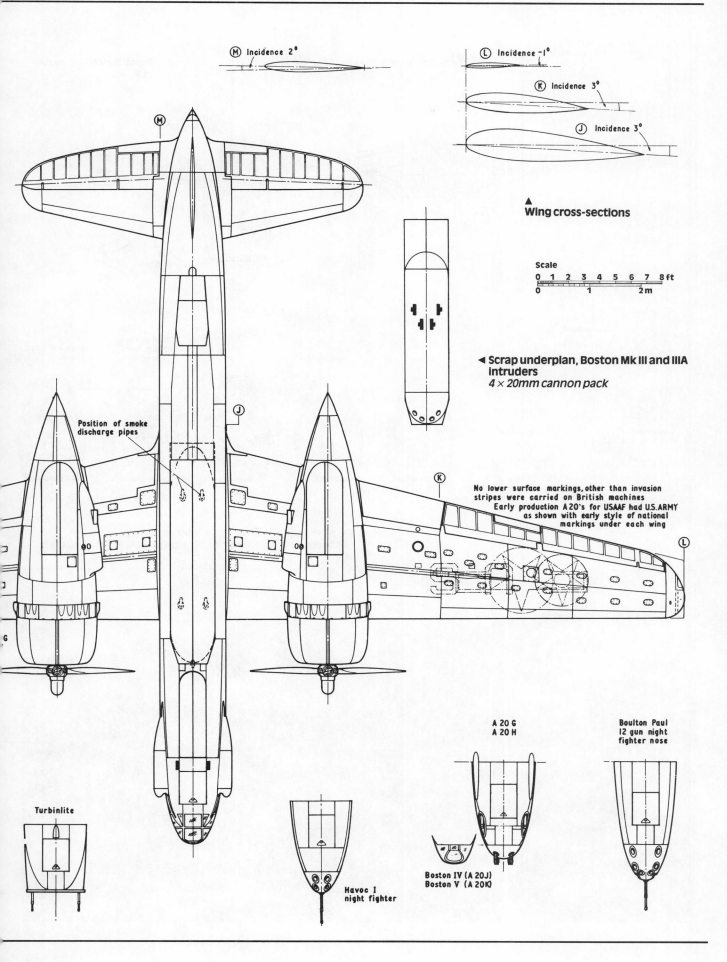

M Incidence 2°

L Incidence -1°

K Incidence 3°

J Incidence 3°

▲ Wing cross-sections

Scale
0 1 2 3 4 5 6 7 8 ft
0   1   2m

◄ Scrap underplan, Boston Mk III and IIIA intruders
4 × 20mm cannon pack

Position of smoke discharge pipes

No lower surface markings, other than invasion stripes were carried on British machines
Early production A20's for USAAF had U.S. ARMY as shown with early style of national markings under each wing

A 20 G
A 20 H

Boulton Paul
12 gun night
fighter nose

Turbinlite

Havoc I
night fighter

Boston IV (A 20J)
Boston V (A 20K)

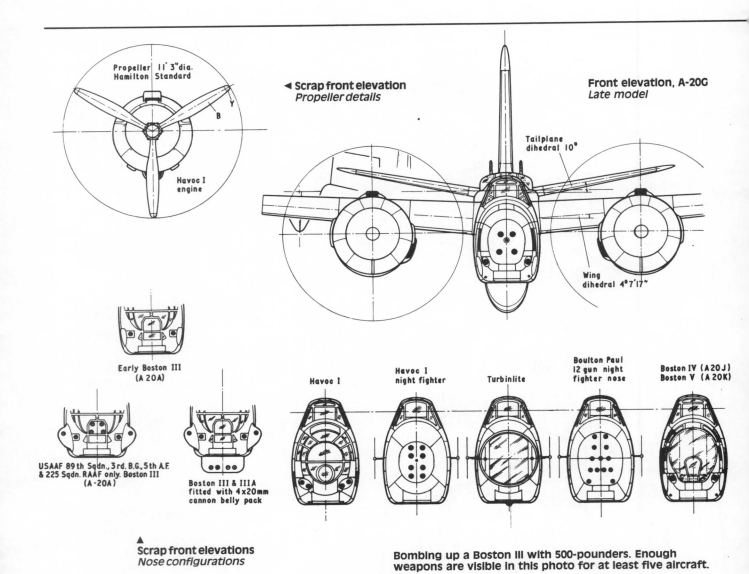

Propeller 11' 3" dia.
Hamilton Standard

Havoc I engine

◀ **Scrap front elevation**
Propeller details

Front elevation, A-20G
Late model

Tailplane dihedral 10°

Wing dihedral 4° 7' 17"

Early Boston III
(A 20A)

USAAF 89th Sqdn., 3rd. B.G., 5th A.F.
& 225 Sqdn. RAAF only. Boston III
(A-20A)

Boston III & IIIA
fitted with 4x20mm
cannon belly pack

Havoc I

Havoc I
night fighter

Turbinlite

Boulton Paul
12 gun night
fighter nose

Boston IV (A20J)
Boston V (A20K)

▲
Scrap front elevations
Nose configurations

Bombing up a Boston III with 500-pounders. Enough
weapons are visible in this photo for at least five aircraft.
▼

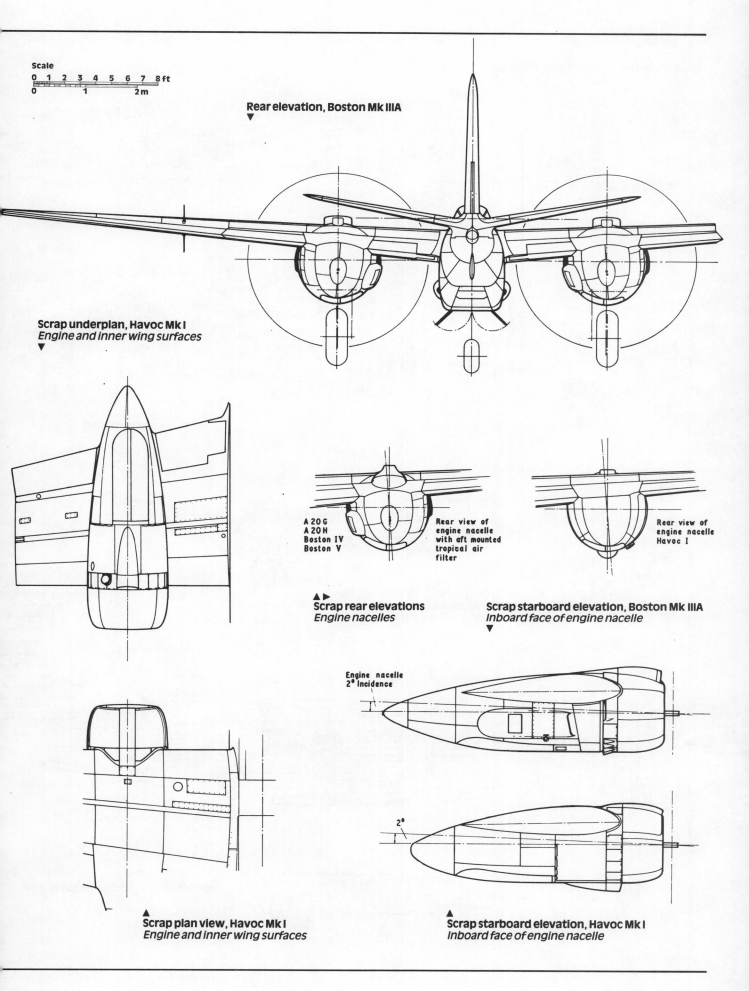

Scale
0 1 2 3 4 5 6 7 8 ft
0 1 2 m

Rear elevation, Boston Mk IIIA

Scrap underplan, Havoc Mk I
Engine and inner wing surfaces

A 20 G
A 20 H
Boston IV
Boston V

Rear view of
engine nacelle
with aft mounted
tropical air
filter

Rear view of
engine nacelle
Havoc I

Scrap rear elevations
Engine nacelles

Scrap starboard elevation, Boston Mk IIIA
Inboard face of engine nacelle

Engine nacelle
2° Incidence

2°

Scrap plan view, Havoc Mk I
Engine and inner wing surfaces

Scrap starboard elevation, Havoc Mk I
Inboard face of engine nacelle

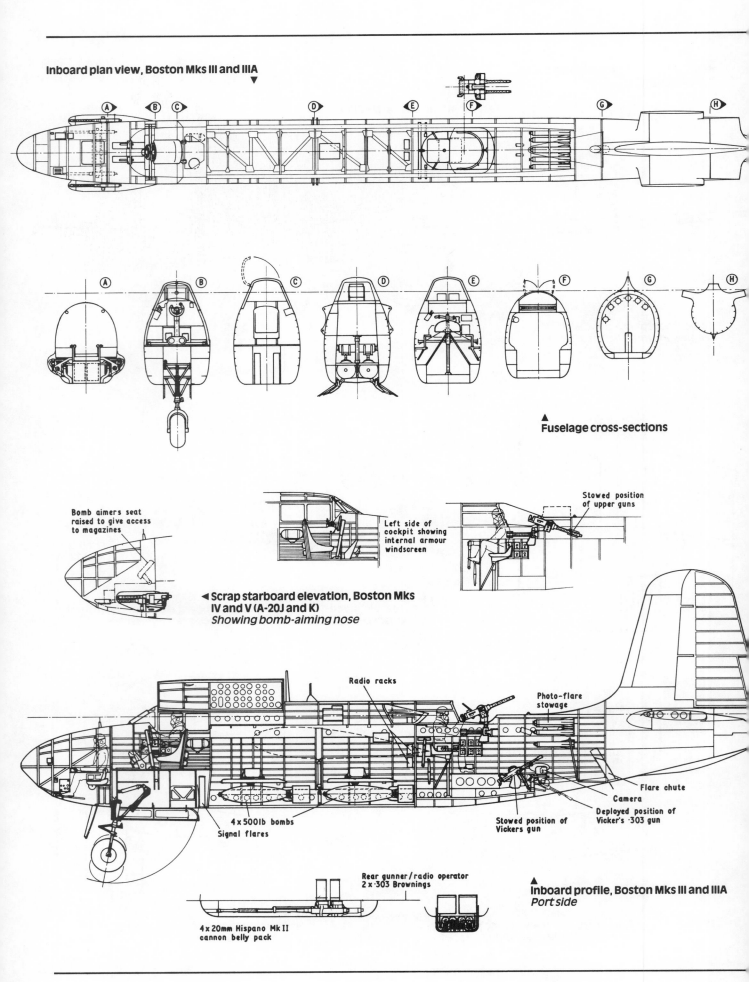

Inboard plan view, Boston Mks III and IIIA

Fuselage cross-sections

Bomb aimers seat
raised to give access
to magazines

Left side of
cockpit showing
internal armour
windscreen

Stowed position
of upper guns

◄ **Scrap starboard elevation, Boston Mks
IV and V (A-20J and K)**
Showing bomb-aiming nose

Radio racks

Photo-flare
stowage

Flare chute

Camera

Deployed position of
Vicker's ·303 gun

Stowed position of
Vickers gun

4 x 500lb bombs

Signal flares

Rear gunner/radio operator
2 x ·303 Brownings

4 x 20mm Hispano Mk II
cannon belly pack

▲ **Inboard profile, Boston Mks III and IIIA**
Port side

A-20G Havoc with four-cannon nose installation. ▶

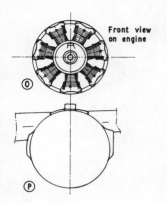

Front view on engine

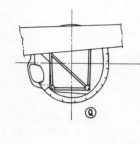 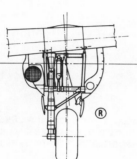 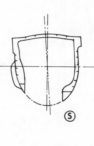 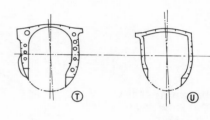

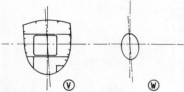

▲ **Nacelle cross-sections**

Line of rear mounted tropical air filter fairing

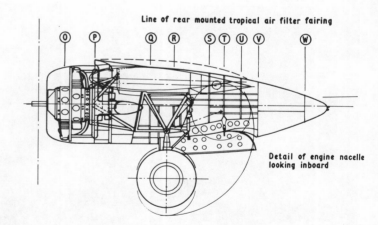

Detail of engine nacelle looking inboard

Detail of engine nacelle looking outboard

Front mounted tropical air filter

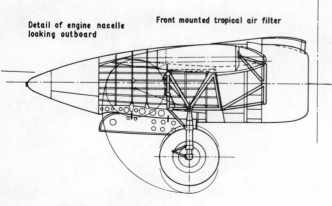

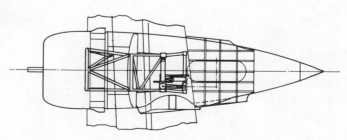

▲▶ **Inboard profiles**
Engine nacelles

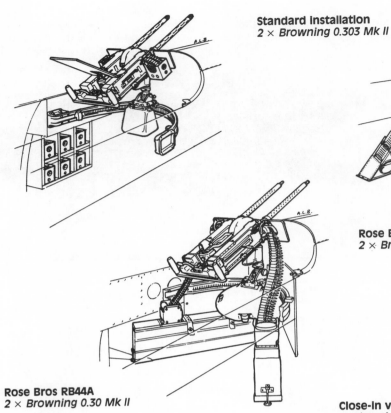

Standard installation
2 × Browning 0.303 Mk II

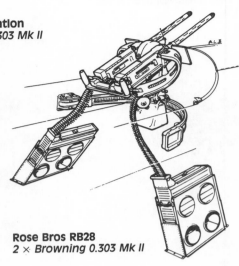

Rose Bros RB28
2 × Browning 0.303 Mk II

Armament variations

Rose Bros RB44A
2 × Browning 0.30 Mk II

Close-in view of an A-20A. The DB-7 design was a private venture by Douglas and was originally developed in response to a French proposal.
▼

Yakovlev Yak-9

Country of origin: USSR.
Type: Single-seat, land-based close-support fighter or (-9U) interceptor and fighter-bomber.
Dimensions: Wing span 32ft 9¾in *10.00m*; length 28ft 0½in *8.55m*, (-9U) 28ft 6½in *8.70m*; height 8ft 0in *2.44m*; wing area 185.7 sq ft *17.25m²*.
Weights: Empty (-9U) 5102lb *2315kg*; take-off (-9D) 6856lb *3115kg*, (-9DD) 7273lb *3300kg*, (-9U) 6943lb *3240kg*, (-9P) 6987lb *3170kg*; loaded 6332lb *2873kg*.
Powerplant: One Klimov M-105PF V12, liquid-cooled piston engine rated at

1260hp, (-9U, -9P) VK-107A rated at 1620hp.
Performance: Maximum speed 368mph *592kph* at 9850ft *3000m*, (-9D, -9DD) 373mph *600kph* at 11,500ft *3500m*, (-9U) 435mph *700kph* at 18,050ft *5500m*, (-9P) 415mph *668kph* at 16,400ft *5000m*; time to 16,400ft *5000m*, 4.9min, (-9U) 3.6min; service ceiling 32,800ft *10,000m*, (-9U) 34,450ft *10,500m*, (-9P) 39,400ft *12,000m*; range 565 miles *910km*, (-9D) 807 miles *1300km*, (-9DD) 1366 miles *2200km*, (-9T) 509 miles *820km*, (-9U, -9P) 547 miles *880km*.

Armament: One fixed 20mm ShVak cannon and one fixed 12.7mm UBS machine gun, (-9D, -9DD) one fixed 20mm MPSh cannon and one fixed 12.7mm UBS machine gun, (-9T) one fixed 37mm Type 11-P-37, 20mm MPSh or 23mm MP-23VV cannon and one fixed 12.7mm UBS machine gun, (-9U, -9P) one fixed 20mm ShVak cannon and two 12.7mm UBS machine guns, plus up to 440lb *200kg* of bombs or rockets.
Service: First flight (-7DI) summer 1942, (-9D, -9T) 1943, (-9U) January 1944; service entry (-9) August 1942, (-9U) late 1944.

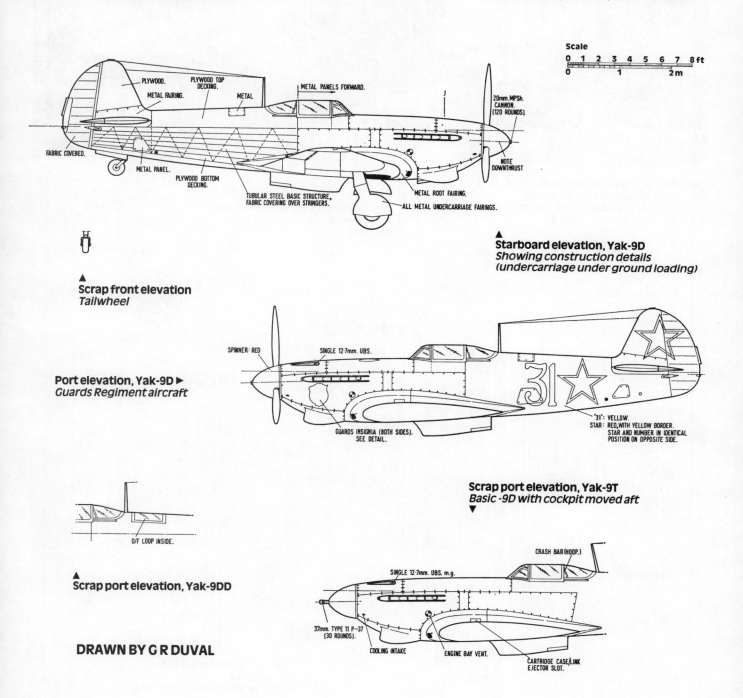

Scale
0 1 2 3 4 5 6 7 8 ft
0 1 2m

Scrap front elevation
Tailwheel

Starboard elevation, Yak-9D
Showing construction details (undercarriage under ground loading)

Port elevation, Yak-9D ▶
Guards Regiment aircraft

Scrap port elevation, Yak-9DD

Scrap port elevation, Yak-9T
Basic -9D with cockpit moved aft
▼

DRAWN BY G R DUVAL

▲
The Yak-3 was generally similar to the -9 though was marginally smaller all round and lacked the latter's chin intake.

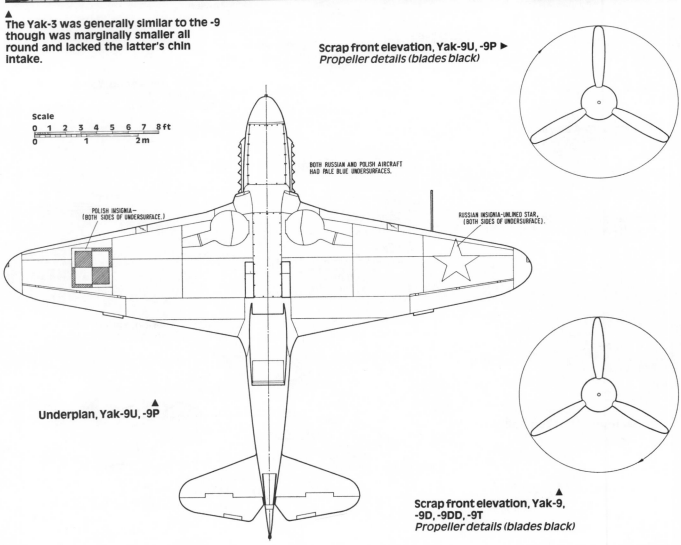

Scrap front elevation, Yak-9U, -9P ▶
Propeller details (blades black)

Scale
0 1 2 3 4 5 6 7 8 ft
0   1   2 m

BOTH RUSSIAN AND POLISH AIRCRAFT
HAD PALE BLUE UNDERSURFACES.

POLISH INSIGNIA—
(BOTH SIDES OF UNDERSURFACE.)

RUSSIAN INSIGNIA—UNLINED STAR,
(BOTH SIDES OF UNDERSURFACE).

Underplan, Yak-9U, -9P ▲

▲
Scrap front elevation, Yak-9, -9D, -9DD, -9T
Propeller details (blades black)

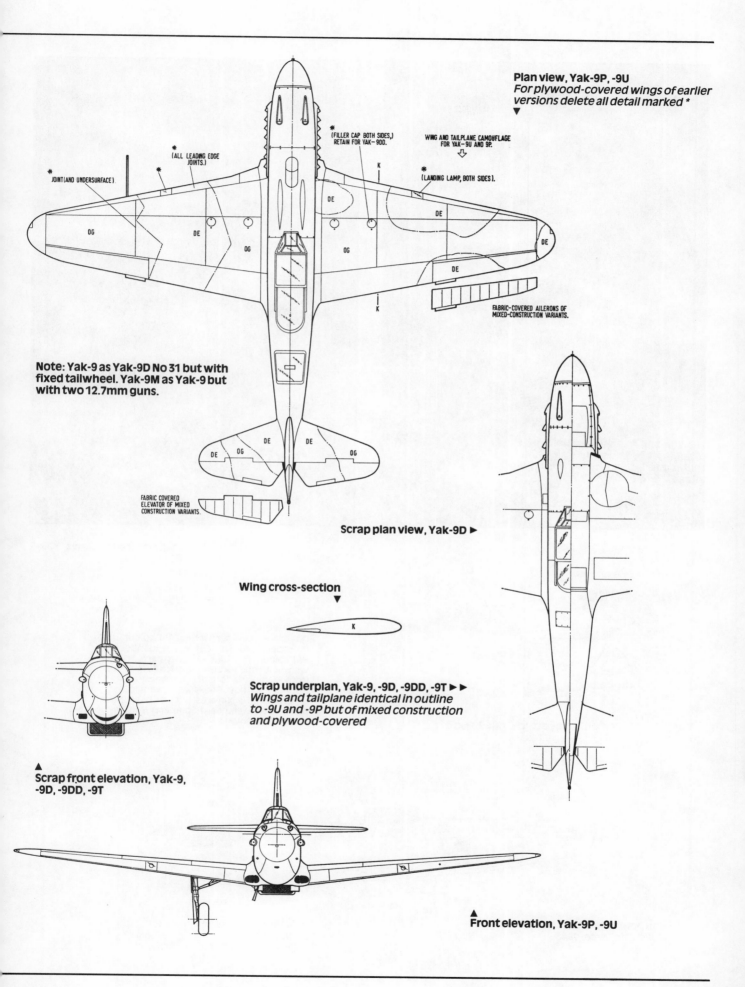

Plan view, Yak-9P, -9U
*For plywood-covered wings of earlier versions delete all detail marked ** ▼

(FILLER CAP BOTH SIDES,)
RETAIN FOR YAK-9DD.

WING AND TAILPLANE CAMOUFLAGE
FOR YAK-9U AND 9P.

*(ALL LEADING EDGE JOINTS.)

*JOINT (AND UNDERSURFACE).

*(LANDING LAMP, BOTH SIDES).

FABRIC-COVERED AILERONS OF
MIXED-CONSTRUCTION VARIANTS.

Note: Yak-9 as Yak-9D No 31 but with fixed tailwheel. Yak-9M as Yak-9 but with two 12.7mm guns.

FABRIC COVERED
ELEVATOR OF MIXED
CONSTRUCTION VARIANTS.

Scrap plan view, Yak-9D ▶

Wing cross-section
▼

Scrap underplan, Yak-9, -9D, -9DD, -9T ▶▶
Wings and tailplane identical in outline to -9U and -9P but of mixed construction and plywood-covered

▲
Scrap front elevation, Yak-9, -9D, -9DD, -9T

▲
Front elevation, Yak-9P, -9U

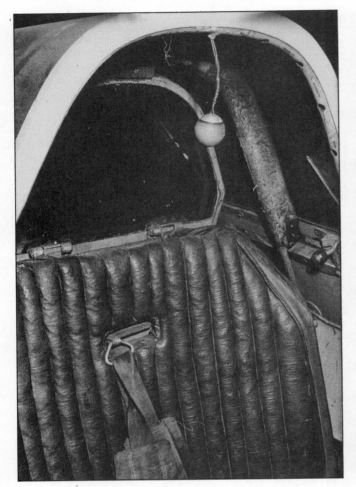

◄◄
Cockpit interior views, Yak-3

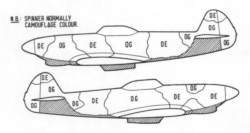

N.B.: SPINNER NORMALLY CAMOUFLAGE COLOUR.

▲
Camouflage pattern, Yak-9D No 31

Colour code

OG – Olive green (similar to USAAF colour used in Europe, 1944); **DE** – Dark Earth (identical to RAF colour); Pale blue – Mix two parts matt white with one part Humbrol No 76 *Hellgrau*.
Note: Many variations of this scheme existed. Prior to 1944 most Yak-9s were overall olive green on upper surfaces, but pale blue under surfaces were standard. Spinner normally camouflage colour.

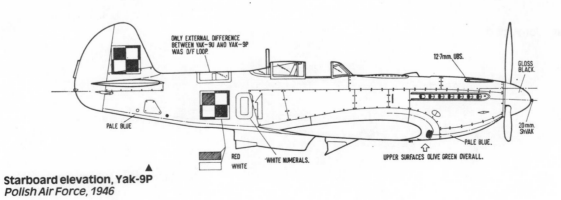

ONLY EXTERNAL DIFFERENCE BETWEEN YAK-9U AND YAK-9P WAS D/F LOOP.

12·7mm. UBS.

GLOSS BLACK.

PALE BLUE

20mm. ShVAK

PALE BLUE.

RED
WHITE

WHITE NUMERALS.

UPPER SURFACES OLIVE GREEN OVERALL.

▲
Starboard elevation, Yak-9P
Polish Air Force, 1946

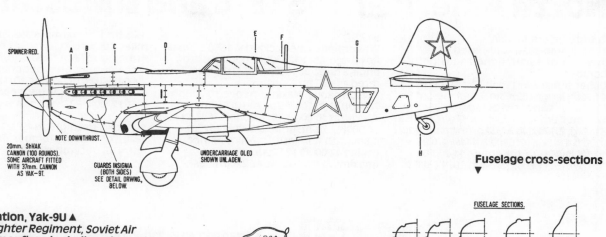

SPINNER:RED.

20mm. ShVAK CANNON (100 ROUNDS). SOME AIRCRAFT FITTED WITH 37mm. CANNON AS YAK–9T.

NOTE DOWNTHRUST.

GUARDS INSIGNIA (BOTH SIDES) SEE DETAIL DRWNG, BELOW.

UNDERCARRIAGE OLEO SHOWN UNLADEN.

Port elevation, Yak-9U ▲
Guards Fighter Regiment, Soviet Air Force (camouflage in similar scheme to Yak-9D, with yellow edging to stars and white numerals)

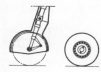

▲
Scrap views, Yak-9P, -9U
Inboard view of undercarriage (other variants similar)

ГВАРДИЯ
CCCP

RED:— FLAG AND STAR.
WHITE:— STAR BACKGROUND.
GOLD:— LAUREL LEAVES, FLAG LETTERING, FLAGSTAFF
TASSELS AND RIBBONS, SCROLL, STAR AND FLAG
EDGING.
'CCCP' ENGRAVED ON SCROLL.

▲
Guards Regiment insignia

Fuselage cross-sections
▼

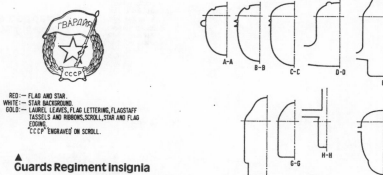

FUSELAGE SECTIONS.

A-A B-B C-C D-D E-E

F-F G-G H-H J-J

Yak-3 close up, showing configuration of canopy. The Yak-9 was developed in parallel to the -3 and shared many of its design features.
▼

North American P-51B, C and D Mustang

Country of origin: USA.
Type: Single-seat, land-based interceptor, escort fighter and fighter-bomber.
Dimensions: Wing span 37ft 0¼in *11.28m*; length 32ft 3in *9.83m*; height 8ft 8in *2.64m*; wing area 233 sq ft *21.65m²*.
Weights: Empty 6840lb *3103kg*, (C) 6985lb *3169kg*, (D) 7125lb *3233kg*; normal loaded 9200lb *4147kg*, (C) 9800lb *4446kg*, (D) 10,100lb *4583kg*; maximum 11,200lb *5082kg*, (C) 11,800lb *5354kg*, (D) 12,100lb

5490kg.
Powerplant: One Packard V-1650-3 (Rolls-Royce Merlin) V12, liquid-cooled piston engine rated at 1620hp, (C, D) V-1650-7 rated at 1695hp.
Performance: Maximum speed 440mph *708kph* at 30,000ft *9145m*, (C) 435mph *700kph* at 30,000ft, (D) 437mph *704kph* at 25,000ft *7620m*; time to 5000ft *1525m*, 1.8min, (C) 1.6min, (D) 1.7min; service ceiling 42,000ft *12,800m*; range (maximum external fuel) 2200 miles

3540km, (C) 2440 miles *3930km*, (D) 2100 miles *3380km*.
Armament: Four fixed 0.5in Browning machine guns plus (optional) up to 2000lb *907kg* of bombs, (D) six fixed 0.5in Browning machine guns plus (optional) up to 2000lb *907kg* of bombs or six 5in *127mm* rockets.
Service: First flight (NA-73X) 26 October 1940, (XP-51B) September 1942; service entry (B) December 1943, (D) 1944.

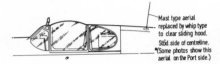

Mast type aerial replaced by whip type to clear sliding hood. Stbd side of centreline. (Some photos show this aerial on the Port side.)

◀ **Scrap port elevation, P-51C**
Showing 'Malcolm' canopy

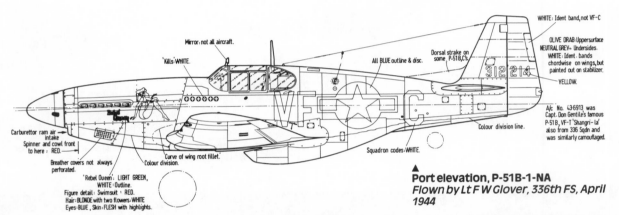

Mirror: not all aircraft.
'Kills' WHITE.
All BLUE outline & disc.
Dorsal strake on some P-51B, C's.
WHITE: Ident band, not VF-C
OLIVE DRAB: Upper surface NEUTRAL GREY: Undersides.
WHITE: Ident. bands chordwise on wings, but painted out on stabilizer.
YELLOW.
A/c No. 43-6913 was Capt. Don Gentile's famous P-51B, VF-T 'Shangri-la' also from 336 Sqdn and was similarly camouflaged.
Colour division line.
Squadron codes: WHITE.
Carburettor ram air intake
Spinner and cowl front to here: RED.
Breather covers not always perforated.
Curve of wing root fillet.
Colour division.
'Rebel Queen': LIGHT GREEN, WHITE: Outline.
Figure detail: Swimsuit: RED.
Hair: BLONDE with two flowers: WHITE
Eyes: BLUE, Skin: FLESH with highlights.

▲ **Port elevation, P-51B-1-NA**
Flown by Lt F W Glover, 336th FS, April 1944

P-51B-1-NA, the first production Mustang variant with a Merlin engine. The powerplant was built under licence by Packard.
▼

A-36A dive-bomber development of the P-51A (note dive brakes). One only was supplied to the RAF.►

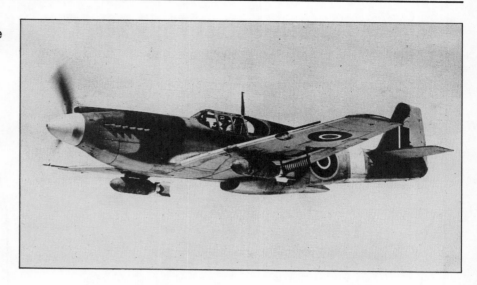

Scrap port elevation, TP-51D
Canopy details, postwar aircraft
▼

There were many 'buddy-seat' wartime conversions on different themes but this one was a TEMCO mod. The USAAF contracted for 15 F-51D's to become TF-51D's. Also on the CAVALIER/PIPER Mustang.

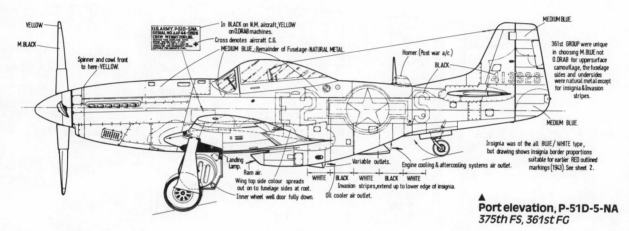

YELLOW

M.BLACK

Spinner and cowl front to here : YELLOW.

U.S.ARMY. P-51O-5NA. SERIAL NO.AAF 44-0926 CREW WEIGHT 200 LBS.

In BLACK on N.M. aircraft, YELLOW on O.DRAB machines.
Cross denotes aircraft C.G.
MEDIUM BLUE.; Remainder of Fuselage : NATURAL METAL.

Homer. (Post war a/c.)

BLACK.

MEDIUM BLUE

413926

361st GROUP were unique in choosing M.BLUE not O.DRAB for uppersurface camouflage, the fuselage sides and undersides were natural metal except for insignia & Invasion stripes.

MEDIUM BLUE.

Landing Lamp.

Ram air.

Wing top side colour spreads out on to fuselage sides at root.

Inner wheel well door fully down.

Variable outlets.

Engine cooling & aftercooling systems air outlet.

WHITE   BLACK   WHITE   BLACK   WHITE

Invasion stripes, extend up to lower edge of insignia.

Oil cooler air outlet.

Insignia was of the all BLUE/WHITE type, but drawing shows insignia border proportions suitable for earlier RED outlined markings (1943). See sheet 2.

▲ Port elevation, P-51D-5-NA
375th FS, 361st FG

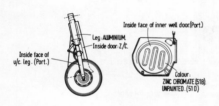

Inside face of inner well door(Port.)

Leg : ALUMINIUM.
Inside door : Z/C.

Inside face of u/c. leg. (Port.)

Colour : ZINC CHROMATE.(51B.) UNPAINTED. (51D)

▲ Scrap views
Undercarriage details

Colour notes

Early P-51Bs and Cs supplied to the USAAF in the UK were finished Olive Drab on upper surfaces and Medium Grey on the undersides, the demarcation line being uneven. Serials used only the last numeral of the year prefix (thus 1943-built aircraft no 12214 had serial 312214); these serials were applied to each side of the fin in yellow. Identification markings were the US insignia 'star and bar' outlined in red, soon superseded by the all-blue type. Mustangs carried chordwise white bands on wings and stabilisers and occasionally across the fin and rudder. These bands were black on

later natural metal aircraft and in turn gave way to Allied invasion markings of black and white stripes on fuselage and wings. The upper surfaces of aircraft with invasion stripes were painted either OD or Medium Blue to make them less conspicuous on the ground after the invasion period.

Many photos show P-51s (mostly B and C variants) with the white portions of the fuselage stars overpainted in a pale grey, to a USAAF T.O. AN-1-9a (June 1943), only to be ignored on the wings of the 361st's Medium Blue aircraft.

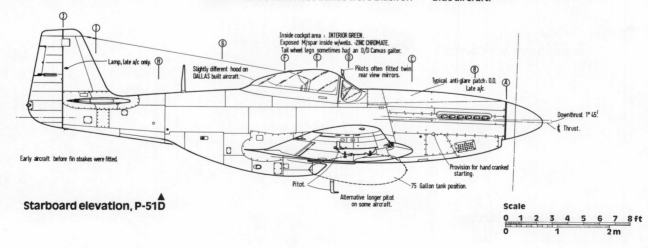

Lamp, late a/c only.

Inside cockpit area : INTERIOR GREEN.
Exposed M/spar inside w/wells. : ZINC CHROMATE.
Tail wheel legs sometimes had an O/D Canvas gaiter.

Slightly different hood on DALLAS built aircraft.

Pilots often fitted twin rear view mirrors.

Typical anti-glare patch : O.D. Late a/c.

Downthrust 1° 45'

Thrust.

Provision for hand cranked starting.

Early aircraft before fin strakes were fitted.

Pitot.

Alternative longer pitot on some aircraft.

75 Gallon tank position.

▲ Starboard elevation, P-51D

Scale

0 1 2 3 4 5 6 7 8 ft

0   1   2 m

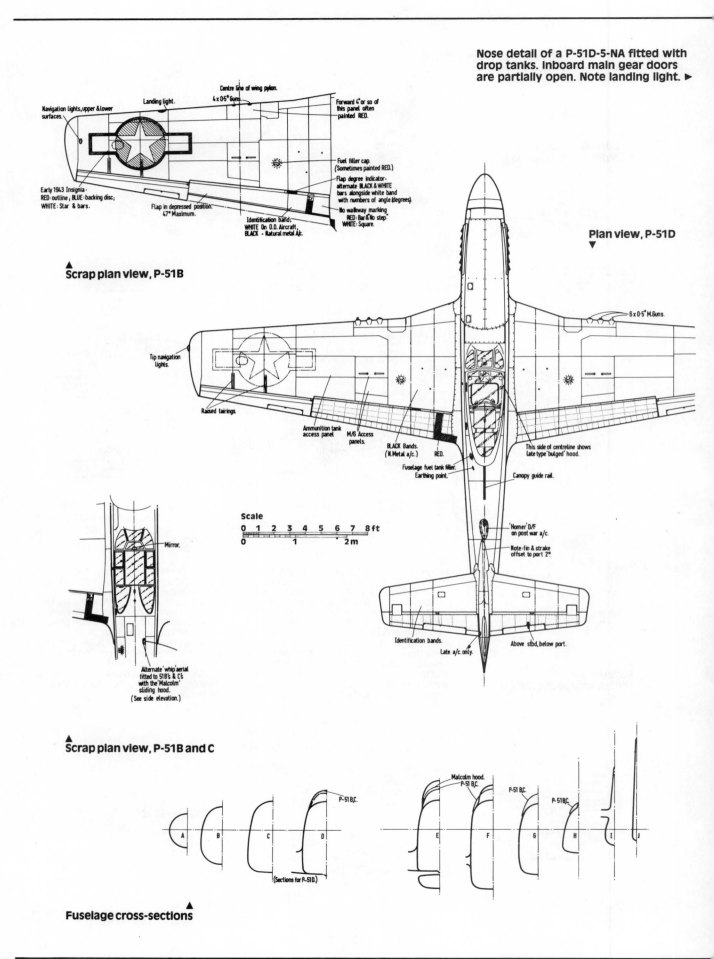

Nose detail of a P-51D-5-NA fitted with drop tanks. Inboard main gear doors are partially open. Note landing light. ▶

Navigation lights, upper & lower surfaces.

Landing light.

Centre line of wing pylon.
4 x 0·5" Guns

Forward 4" or so of this panel often painted RED.

Fuel filler cap. (Sometimes painted RED.)

Flap degree indicator; alternate BLACK & WHITE bars alongside white band with numbers of angle (degrees).

No walkway marking RED: Bar & No step. WHITE: Square.

Early 1943 Insignia; RED: outline; BLUE: backing disc; WHITE: Star & bars.

Flap in depressed position. 47° Maximum.

Identification band; WHITE On O.D. Aircraft, BLACK - Natural metal A/c.

▲ Scrap plan view, P-51B

Plan view, P-51D ▼

6 x 0·5" M.Guns.

Tip navigation lights.

Raised fairings.

Ammunition tank access panel

M/G Access panels.

BLACK Bands. (N.Metal a/c.)

RED.

This side of centreline shows Late type 'bulged' hood.

Fuselage fuel tank filler. Earthing point.

Canopy guide rail.

Mirror.

Scale
0 1 2 3 4 5 6 7 8 ft
0 1 2 m

'Homer' D/F on post war a/c.

Note: fin & strake offset to port 2°

Alternate 'whip' aerial fitted to 51B's & C's with the 'Malcolm' sliding hood. (See side elevation.)

Identification bands. Late a/c. only.

Above stbd, below port.

▲ Scrap plan view, P-51B and C

Malcolm hood.
P-51 B,C.

P-51 B,C.

P-51 B,C.

P-51 B,C.

A B C D E F G H I J

(Sections for P-51D.)

Fuselage cross-sections ▲

Underplan, P-51D
P-51B and C generally similar
▼

Wing cross-sections
▼

Tip.

Root.

K-K.

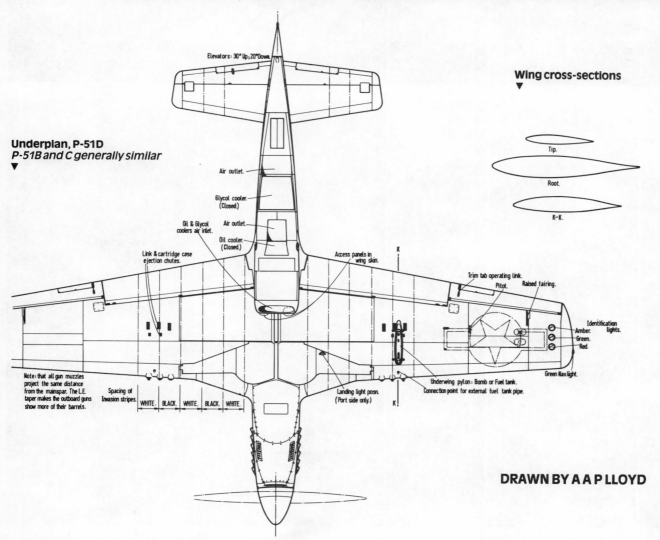

Elevators: 30° Up; 20° Down.

Air outlet.

Glycol cooler.
(Closed.)

Oil & Glycol
coolers air inlet.

Air outlet.

Oil cooler.
(Closed.)

Link & cartridge case
ejection chutes.

Access panels in
wing skin.

Trim tab operating link.

Pitot.

Raised fairing.

Identification
lights.
Amber.
Green.
Red.

Green Nav light.

Note: that all gun muzzles
project the same distance
from the mainspar. The L.E.
taper makes the outboard guns
show more of their barrels.

Spacing of
Invasion stripes.

| WHITE. | BLACK. | WHITE. | BLACK. | WHITE. |

Landing light posn.
(Port side only.)

Underwing pylon: Bomb or Fuel tank.
Connection point for external fuel tank pipe.

DRAWN BY A A P LLOYD

◄ The P-51D featured a full 'bubble' canopy, dramatically improving the pilot's field of view. This well-stained example is in typical natural metal finish.

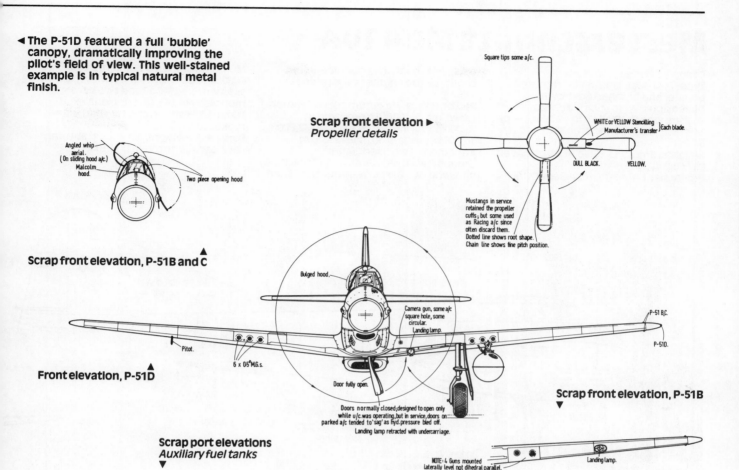

Angled whip aerial.
(On sliding hood a/c.)
Malcolm hood.
Two piece opening hood

Scrap front elevation, P-51B and C ▲

Scrap front elevation ►
Propeller details

Square tips some a/c.

WHITE or YELLOW Stencilling } Each blade.
Manufacturer's transfer

DULL BLACK.   YELLOW.

Mustangs in service retained the propeller cuffs; but some used as Racing a/c since often discard them.
Dotted line shows root shape.
Chain line shows fine pitch position.

Bulged hood.

Camera gun, some a/c square hole, some circular.
Landing lamp.

P-51 B,C.

P-51D.

Front elevation, P-51D ▲

Pitot.

6 x 0.5" M.G.s.

Door fully open.

Doors normally closed; designed to open only while u/c. was operating, but in service, doors on parked a/c tended to 'sag' as hyd. pressure bled off.
Landing lamp retracted with undercarriage.

Scrap front elevation, P-51B ▼

NOTE: 4 Guns mounted laterally level **not** dihedral parallel.
Landing lamp.

Scrap port elevations
Auxiliary fuel tanks ▼

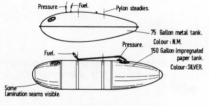

Pressure.   Fuel.   Pylon steadies.

75 Gallon metal tank.
Colour : N.M.

Pressure.
Fuel.

150 Gallon impregnated paper tank.
Colour : SILVER.

Some lamination seams visible.

Connections to feed lines were made in rubber hose to be easily 'breakable' when the tank was jettisonned.

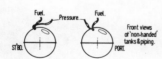

Fuel.   Pressure.   Fuel.

Front views of 'non-handed' tanks & piping.

ST'BD.   PORT.

Scrap front elevations ▲
'Non-handed' tanks and piping

◄ P-51D with 2.5in bazooka tubes. The fin fillet featured on this aircraft was not present on early Ds. Note DF loop aft of aerial mast.

Mustang cockpit interior, showing 'spade' type handgrip on control column and neat panel layout. ►

Messerschmitt Me 410A

Country of origin: Germany.
Type: Two-seat, land-based fighter-bomber and bomber-destroyer.
Dimensions: Wing span 53ft 7¾in *16.35m*; length 40ft 11¼in *12.48m*; height 14ft 0½in *4.28m*; wing area 389.65 sq ft *36.2m²*.
Weights: Empty 13,550lb *6148kg*; loaded 23,500lb *10,662kg*.
Powerplant: Two Daimler-Benz DB 603A

twelve-cylinder, inverted-vee, liquid-cooled piston engines each rated at 1750hp.
Performance: Maximum speed 388mph *625kph* at 22,000ft *6700m*; time to 22,000ft 10.7min; service ceiling 32,800ft *10,000m*; range 1450 miles *2335km*.
Armament: Two fixed 20mm MG 151 cannon, two fixed 7.9mm MG 17 machine guns and two barbette-mounted 13mm

MG 131 machine guns, plus up to 4400lb *2000kg* of bombs, (A-1/U2) four fixed MG 151, two fixed MG 17 and two barbette-mounted MG 131, (A-1/U4) one fixed 50mm BK5 cannon and two barbette-mounted MG 131.
Service: First flight (Me 410V1) autumn 1942; service entry (A-1) January 1943.

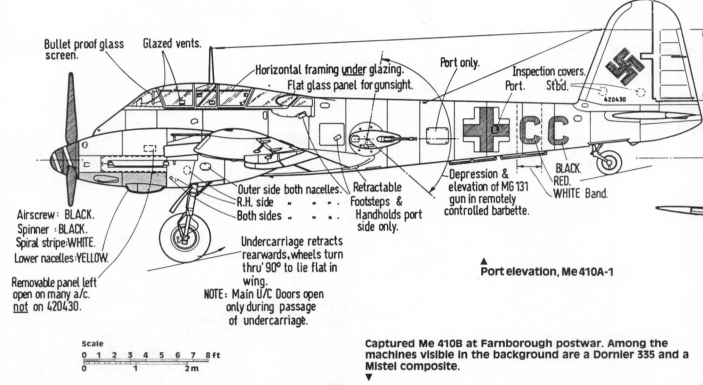

Bullet proof glass screen.
Glazed vents.
Horizontal framing <u>under</u> glazing.
Flat glass panel for gunsight.
Port only.
Inspection covers.
Port. St'b'd.
420430
Fa

Airscrew: BLACK.
Spinner: BLACK.
Spiral stripe: WHITE.
Lower nacelles: YELLOW.

Removable panel left open on many a/c. <u>not</u> on 420430.

Outer side both nacelles.
R.H. side " " " .
Both sides " " " .

Retractable Footsteps & Handholds port side only.

Depression & elevation of MG 131 gun in remotely controlled barbette.

BLACK. RED. WHITE Band.

Undercarriage retracts rearwards, wheels turn thru' 90° to lie flat in wing.
NOTE: Main U/C Doors open only during passage of undercarriage.

▲
Port elevation, Me 410A-1

Scale
0 1 2 3 4 5 6 7 8 ft
0   1   2 m

Captured Me 410B at Farnborough postwar. Among the machines visible in the background are a Dornier 335 and a Mistel composite.
▼

Air intake for cockpit heating.

Bomb door pivot line.

▲
Scrap starboard elevation, Me 410A-1

Scrap front elevation ▶
VDM airscrew

7·9mm MG 17 Guns.   20mm MG 151/20 Guns.

**▼
Front elevation, Me 410A-1**

Bomb bay doors.

Spent cartridge chutes.

Aileron mass balances.
Radiator.
Air intake.
Exhaust.

**Scrap views, Me 410A-3
▼**

Colour notes

Upper surfaces of wings, tailplane and nacelles – Splinter camouflage in *Schwarzgrün 70* (black-green) and *Dunkelgrün 71* (dark green), with sharply defined colour divisions. All undersurfaces – *Hellblau 65* (light blue). Fuselage, fin and rudder – *RLM Grau 02* (greenish-grey) over *Hellblau 65*, almost solid on top, mottled over *65* on sides, mottle becoming progressively lighter down to the *65* undersurfaces.

Note: Colour scheme and markings for Wk Nr 420430 are based on the machine as preserved at RAF Cosford; it has not been possible to confirm whether they are correct as at the time of capture.

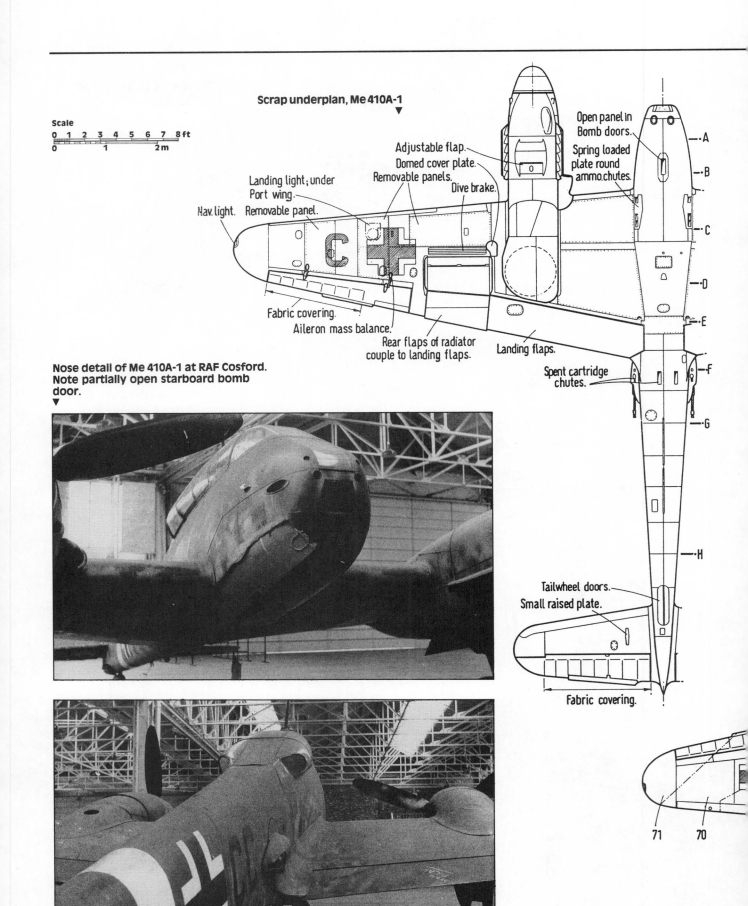

Scrap underplan, Me 410A-1
▼

Scale

0 1 2 3 4 5 6 7 8 ft
0   1   2 m

Adjustable flap.

Domed cover plate.
Removable panels.

Dive brake.

Open panel in
Bomb doors.

Spring loaded
plate round
ammo.chutes.

Landing light; under
Port wing.
Removable panel.

Nav. light.

Fabric covering.

Aileron mass balance.

Rear flaps of radiator
couple to landing flaps.

Landing flaps.

Spent cartridge
chutes.

— A

— B

— C

— D

— E

— F

— G

— H

Tailwheel doors.
Small raised plate.

Fabric covering.

**Nose detail of Me 410A-1 at RAF Cosford.
Note partially open starboard bomb
door.**
▼

71   70

◄ **Rear view of Me 410A-1 shows aft-
facing panels in canopy and location of
starboard barbette to advantage.**

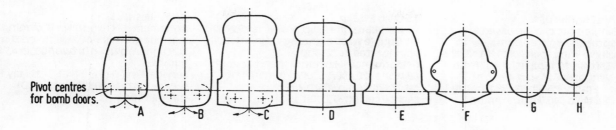

Pivot centres
for bomb doors.

A   B   C   D   E   F   G   H

▲ **Fuselage cross-sections**

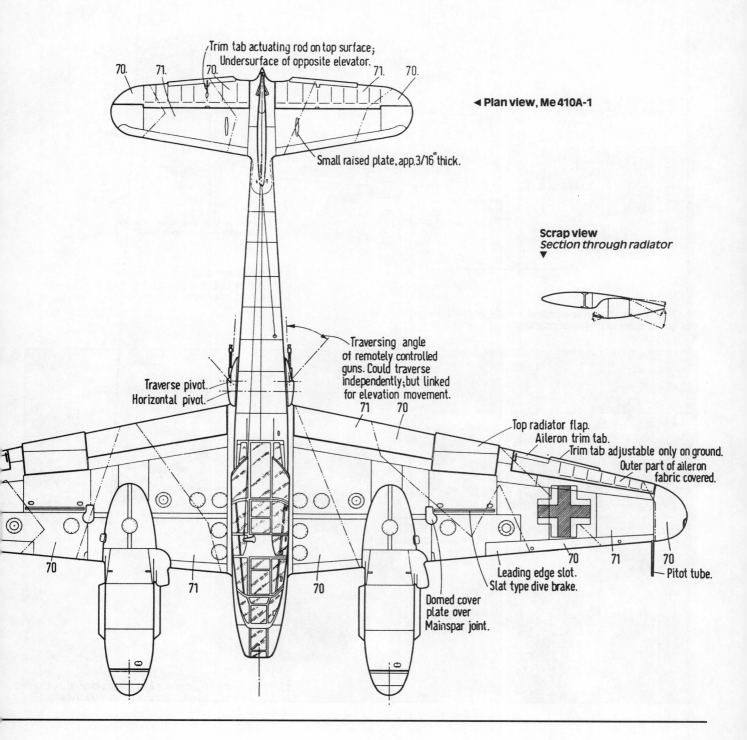

Trim tab actuating rod on top surface;
Undersurface of opposite elevator.

70.   71.   70.   71.   70.

◀ **Plan view, Me 410A-1**

Small raised plate, app. 3/16" thick.

Scrap view
Section through radiator
▼

Traversing angle
of remotely controlled
guns. Could traverse
independently; but linked
for elevation movement.

71   70

Traverse pivot.
Horizontal pivot.

Top radiator flap.
Aileron trim tab.
Trim tab adjustable only on ground.
Outer part of aileron
fabric covered.

70   71

70   71   70

70

Leading edge slot.
Slat type dive brake.

Pitot tube.

Domed cover
plate over
Mainspar joint.

Chance Vought F4U-1 Corsair

Country of origin: USA.
Type: Single-seat, carrier-based interceptor and fighter-bomber.
Dimensions: Wing span 40ft 11in *12.47m*; length 33ft 4in *10.16m*; height 15ft 1in *4.60m*; wing area 314 sq ft *19.17m²*.
Weights: Empty 8695lb *3945kg*; normal loaded 12,040lb *5463kg*; maximum

13,120lb *5953kg*.
Powerplant: One Pratt & Whitney R2800-8W Double Wasp eighteen-cylinder radial engine rated at 2250hp.
Performance: Maximum speed 425mph *684kph* at 20,000ft *6100m*; initial climb rate 3120ft/min *905m/min*; service ceiling 37,000ft *11,280m*; range

1015 miles *1635km*.
Armament: Six fixed 0.5in Browning machine guns or (-1C) four fixed 20mm M2 cannon, plus (-1D) two 1000lb *454kg* bombs.
Service: First flight (XF4U-1) 29 May 1940; service entry (-1A) July 1942, (-1D) summer 1944.

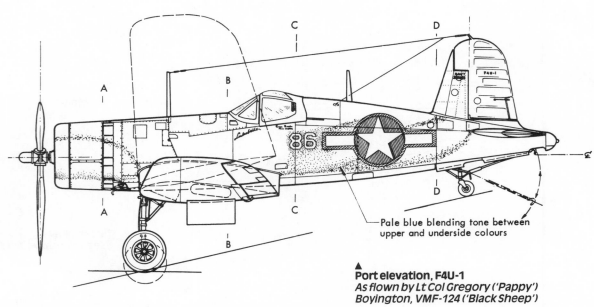

—Pale blue blending tone between upper and underside colours

▲
Port elevation, F4U-1
As flown by Lt Col Gregory ('Pappy') Boyington, VMF-124 ('Black Sheep')

The F4U-4 was the final wartime model of the Corsair. This -B variant is seen in postwar markings.
▼

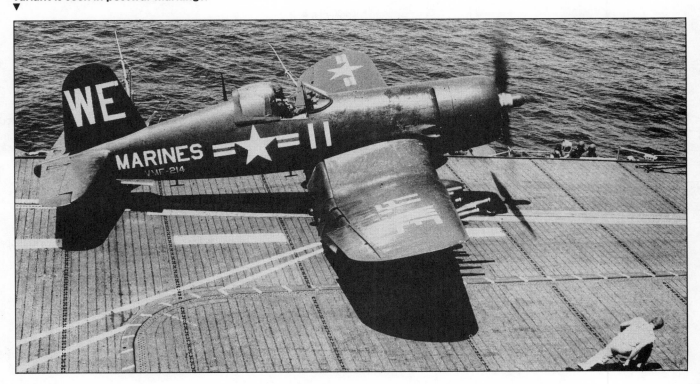

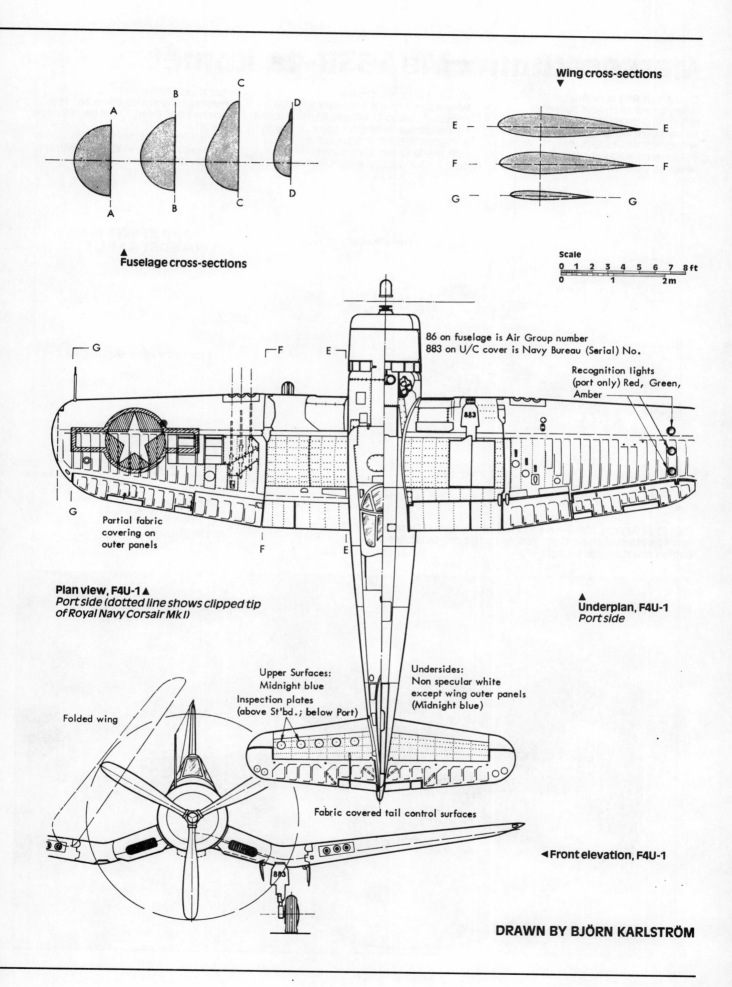

Wing cross-sections

E — E
F — F
G — G

▲ **Fuselage cross-sections**

Scale
0 1 2 3 4 5 6 7 8 ft
0 1 2m

86 on fuselage is Air Group number
883 on U/C cover is Navy Bureau (Serial) No.

Recognition lights
(port only) Red, Green,
Amber

Partial fabric
covering on
outer panels

Plan view, F4U-1 ▲
*Port side (dotted line shows clipped tip
of Royal Navy Corsair Mk I)*

▲ **Underplan, F4U-1**
Port side

Upper Surfaces:
Midnight blue

Inspection plates
(above St'bd.; below Port)

Undersides:
Non specular white
except wing outer panels
(Midnight blue)

Folded wing

Fabric covered tail control surfaces

◄ **Front elevation, F4U-1**

DRAWN BY BJÖRN KARLSTRÖM

Messerschmitt Me 163B-1a Komet

Country of origin: Germany.
Type: Single-seat, land-based point defence interceptor.
Dimensions: Wing span 30ft 7¼in *9.33m*; length 19ft 2¼in *5.85m*; height 9ft 0½in *2.75m*; wing area 199.1 sq ft *18.5m²*.
Weights: Empty 4200lb *1905kg*;

maximum 9500lb *4310kg*.
Powerplant: One Walter HWK 509A-2 rocket motor of 3750lb *1700kg* thrust.
Performance: Maximum speed 596mph *960kph* at 20,000ft *6100m*; initial climb rate 16,000ft/min *4875m/min*; service ceiling 39,400ft *12,000m*; maximum

endurance 7.5min.
Armament: Two fixed 20mm MG 151 cannon or two fixed 30mm MK 108 cannon.
Service: First flight (Me 163V1, unpowered) spring 1941; service entry (B-1) May 1944.

DRAWN BY IAN R STAIR
TRACED BY A A P LLOYD

Starboard elevation, Me 163B-1a ▼

METAL COVERED TIP.
FABRIC COVERED RUDDER.
METAL COVERED TAB.
ARMOUR GLASS SCREEN.
CANOPY HINGES.
EXTRA FAIRING ON AIRSCREW BOSS.
15mm ARMOUR PLATE NOSE CONE.
TRUE CIRCULAR FUSELAGE SHOWN AS DOTTED LINES TOP & BOTTOM.
STENCILLED WORDING SHOWN THUS.
TAILWHEEL WITH FULL FAIRING IN LOWERED POSITION.
VENTS IN TAIL CONE, BOTH SIDES ON I.W.M. & CRANFIELD AIRCRAFT.

Front elevation, Me 163B-1a ▼

90mm ARMOURED GLASS SCREEN.
30mm MK 108 CANNON. (EACH SIDE.)
TRAILING EDGE LINE.
PITOT.
WING TIP SKID.
SKID RETRACTED
SKID LOWERED
NOTE: AXLE AND WHEELS WERE DROPPED AFTER TAKE-OFF.

Me 163 at Dayton, this view showing the unique tailless configuration of the design. Walter rocket motor is posed behind the starboard wing.
▼

Plan view, Me 163B-1a
▼

▲
Komet 191316 displayed in London's Science Museum and here affording a good view of the jettisonable undercarriage.

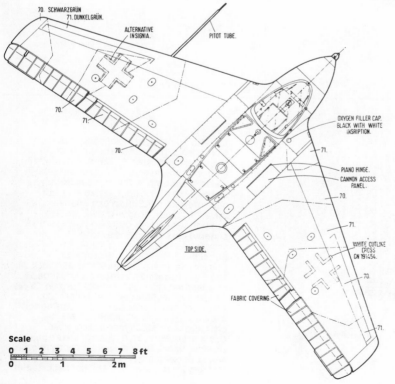

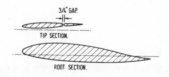

3/4" GAP.

TIP SECTION.

ROOT SECTION.

SECTION THROUGH SLOT AND FLAP.

▲
Wing cross-sections

Scale
0 1 2 3 4 5 6 7 8 ft
0   1   2 m

Colour notes
Undersides of wings and fuselage – *Hellblau 65* (light blue). Sides and top of fuselage and tail surfaces oversprayed with *RLM Grau 02* (light grey) in mottle pattern. Top surface of wings – 'Splinter' pattern camouflage in *Dunkelgrün 71* (dark green) and *Schwarzgrün 70* (black-green). Interior details – RLM Grau 02 (light grey).

Port elevation, Me 163B-1a ▼

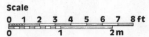

Scale

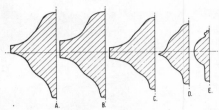

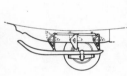

YELLOW NOSE.
BLACK RING.

RED DOTTED RING ON MOST AIRCRAFT; (NOT ON 191454).

BLACK 'T', WHITE DISC.
RED 'C', WHITE SQUARE.
QUICK RELEASE CATCHES.
N° '11': YELLOW, WITH DK. GREY OUTLINE. N° 191454 IN BLACK, THIS SIDE ONLY.

191 454

SMALL 'C' WITHOUT WHITE PANEL ON 191454.
NO WHEEL FAIRING ON 191454. NOTE: Me 163's OFTEN OPERATED WITHOUT THIS FAIRING.

Fuselage cross-sections (approximate) ▲

Scrap views, Me 163B-1a
Undercarriage/skid details ▼

ALTERNATIVE WHEEL FAIRING AND TAIL CONE VENT. NOTE: NO VENTS ON 191454.

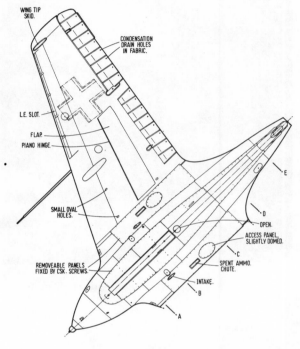

WING TIP SKID.
CONDENSATION DRAIN HOLES IN FABRIC.
L.E. SLOT.
FLAP.
PIANO HINGE.
SMALL OVAL HOLES.
REMOVEABLE PANELS FIXED BY CSK. SCREWS.
E
D
OPEN.
ACCESS PANEL, SLIGHTLY DOMED.
C
SPENT AMMO. CHUTE.
B
INTAKE.
A

Scrap views ▲
Cockpit details, early production aircraft

▲
Underplan, Me 163B-1a

Cockpit details, Me 163B series

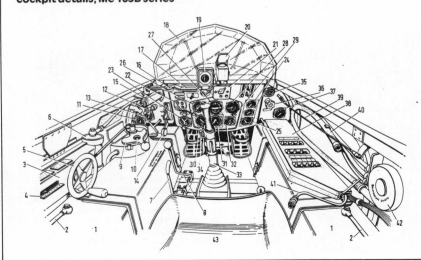

Key
1. 'T-stoff' tank each side of cockpit. 2. Fuel feed pipes. 3. Trim control box. 4. Trim adjustment indicator. 5. Trimmer handwheel. 6. Oil pressure reservoir. 7. Flap selector lever. 8. Flap handpump. 9. Throttle quadrant. 10. Starter switch. 11. Undercarriage system pressure gauge. 12. Undercarriage selector valve. 13. Compressed air gauge. 14. Skid position selector. 15. Quick dump for fuel. 16. Canopy latch. 17. Canopy release. 18. 90mm armour glass. 19. Compass. 20. Revi 16 reflector gun sight. 21. FuG 25a control box. 22. Undercarriage position indicator. 23. Clock. 24. Thrust indicators. 25. Temperature gauge. 26. Air speed indicator. 27. Artificial horizon. 28. Variometer. 29. Fuel contents telltale. 30. Altimeter. 31. RPM counter. 32. Consumption indicator. 33. Control column. 34. MK 108 charging knob. 35. Oxygen indicator. 36. Oxygen regulator. 37. Oxygen pressure gauge. 38. Radio panel. 39. Emergency canopy release. 40. Pilot's oxygen pipe. 41. Helmet/radio lead. 42. Oxygen supply outlet. 43. Seat (adjustable).

Captured Me 163 with wings detached and panels missing shows glimpses of the structure of this very advanced but highly volatile interceptor.

Komet 191659 while at the Institute of Technology at Cranfield, with extemporary wing root fairing panel. Wing slot is evident from this angle.

Hawker Tempest Mks I–VI

Country of origin: Great Britain.
Type: Single-seat, land-based interceptor fighter and fighter-bomber.
Dimensions: Wing span 41ft 0in *12.50m*; length 33ft 7in *10.24m*, (Mk II) 34ft 5in *10.49m*, (Mks V, VI) 33ft 8in *10.26m*; height 16ft 0in *4.88m*, (Mk II) 15ft 6in *4.72m*, (Mks V, VI) 16ft 1in *4.90m*; wing area 310 sq ft *28.8m²*, (Mk II) 303.7 sq ft *28.21m²*, (Mks V, VI) 302 sq ft *28.06m²*.
Powerplant: One Napier Sabre IV 24-cylinder, horizontal-H, liquid-cooled piston engine rated at 2240hp, (Mk II) Bristol Centaurus V or VI eighteen-cylinder radial engine rated at 2520hp, (Mk V) Sabre IIB rated at 2200hp, (Mk VI) Sabre VA rated at 2340hp.
Performance: Maximum speed 466mph *750kph* at 24,500ft *7470m*, (Mk II) 440mph *708kph* at 15,900ft *4850m*, (Mk V) 435mph *700kph* at 17,000ft *5180m*; initial climb rate (Mk II) 4500ft/min *1370m/min*, (Mk V) 4700ft/min *1430m/min*; service ceiling (Mk II) 37,000ft *11,280m*, (Mk V) 36,000ft *10,950m*; range (clean, Mk II) 775 miles *1250km*, (Mk V) 820 miles *1320km*.
Armament: Four fixed 20mm Hispano cannon plus (Mks II, V, VI) two 1000lb *454kg* bombs or eight 60lb *27kg* rocket projectiles.
Service: First flight (prototype Mk V) 2 September 1942, (prototype Mk II) 28 June 1943, (prototype Mk VI) 9 May 1944; service entry (Mk V) April 1944, (Mk II) November 1945.

◀ **Fuselage cross-sections**

Port elevation, Mk I
▼

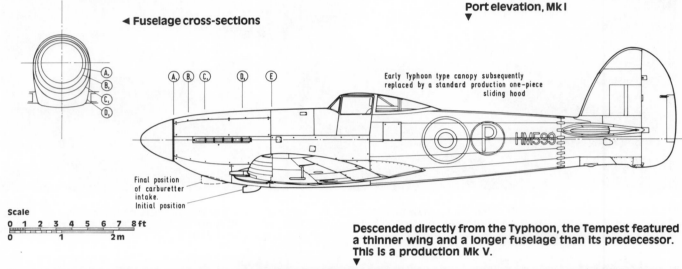

Early Typhoon type canopy subsequently replaced by a standard production one-piece sliding hood

Final position of carburetter intake.
Initial position

Scale

0 1 2 3 4 5 6 7 8 ft
0   1   2m

Descended directly from the Typhoon, the Tempest featured a thinner wing and a longer fuselage than its predecessor. This is a production Mk V.
▼

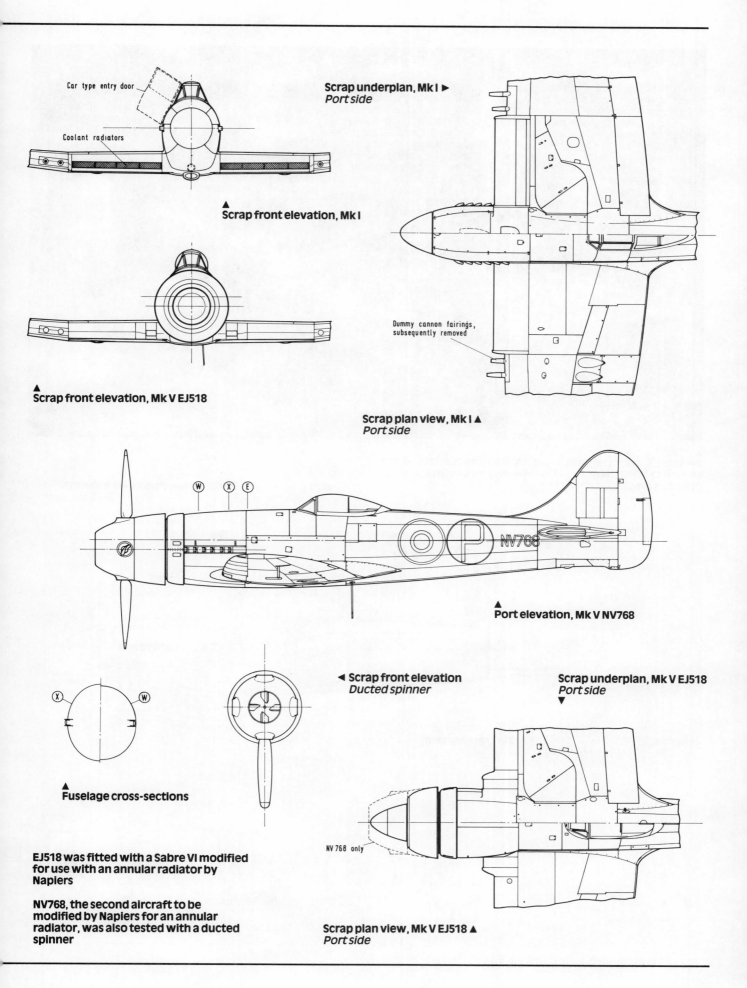

Car type entry door

Coolant radiators

Scrap front elevation, Mk I

Scrap front elevation, Mk V EJ518

Scrap underplan, Mk I ▶
Port side

Dummy cannon fairings, subsequently removed

Scrap plan view, Mk I ▲
Port side

W X E

NV768

Port elevation, Mk V NV768 ▲

X W

Fuselage cross-sections

◀ Scrap front elevation
Ducted spinner

Scrap underplan, Mk V EJ518
Port side
▼

NV 768 only

EJ518 was fitted with a Sabre VI modified for use with an annular radiator by Napiers

NV768, the second aircraft to be modified by Napiers for an annular radiator, was also tested with a ducted spinner

Scrap plan view, Mk V EJ518 ▲
Port side

▲ Tempest II, with Centaurus engine, was just too late to see service in WW2. Here PR747 is receiving its starboard wing prior to completion.

Starboard elevation, Mk V Series II
▼

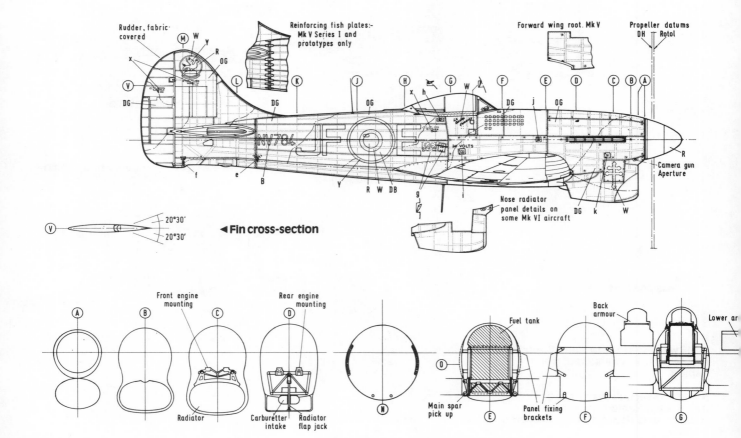

Rudder, fabric covered

Reinforcing fish plates:- Mk V Series I and prototypes only

Forward wing root. Mk V

Propeller datums DH Rotol

Camera gun Aperture

Nose radiator panel details on some Mk VI aircraft

◄ Fin cross-section

20°30'
20°30'

Front engine mounting

Rear engine mounting

Back armour

Fuel tank

Lower ar

Radiator

Carburetter intake

Radiator flap jack

Main spar pick up

Panel fixing brackets

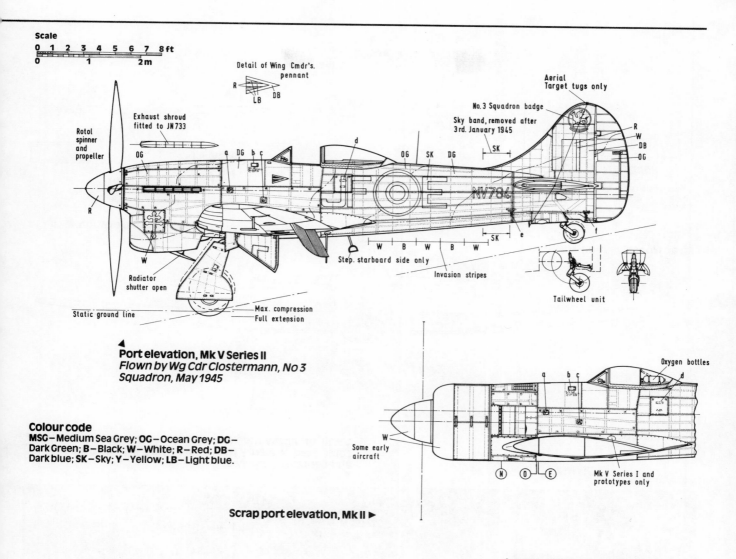

Scale

0 1 2 3 4 5 6 7 8 ft
0 1 2m

Detail of Wing Cmdr's. pennant

R
LB DB

Aerial Target tugs only

No. 3 Squadron badge
Sky band, removed after 3rd. January 1945

Rotol spinner and propeller

Exhaust shroud fitted to JN733

OG

R

DG b c

d

OG SK DG

SK

R
W
DB
OG

JF○E NV786

W

Step. starboard side only

W B W B W

SK

e

f

Radiator shutter open

Invasion stripes

Static ground line

Max. compression
Full extension

Tailwheel unit

◀ **Port elevation, Mk V Series II**
*Flown by Wg Cdr Clostermann, No 3
Squadron, May 1945*

Oxygen bottles

a b c

d

W

Some early aircraft

N O E

Mk V Series I and prototypes only

Colour code
MSG – Medium Sea Grey; **OG** – Ocean Grey; **DG** –
Dark Green; **B** – Black; **W** – White; **R** – Red; **DB** –
Dark blue; **SK** – Sky; **Y** – Yellow; **LB** – Light blue.

Scrap port elevation, Mk II ▶

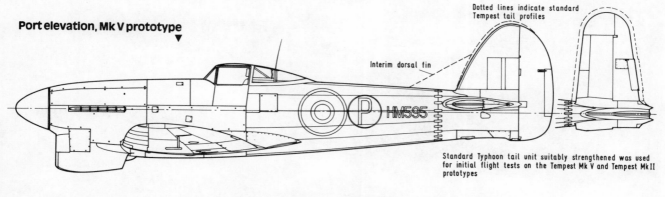

Port elevation, Mk V prototype
▼

Dotted lines indicate standard Tempest tail profiles

Interim dorsal fin

○P HM595

Standard Typhoon tail unit suitably strengthened was used for initial flight tests on the Tempest Mk V and Tempest Mk II prototypes

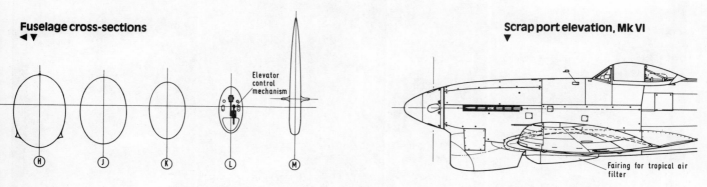

Fuselage cross-sections
◀▼

Elevator control mechanism

H J K L M

Scrap port elevation, Mk VI
▼

Fairing for tropical air filter

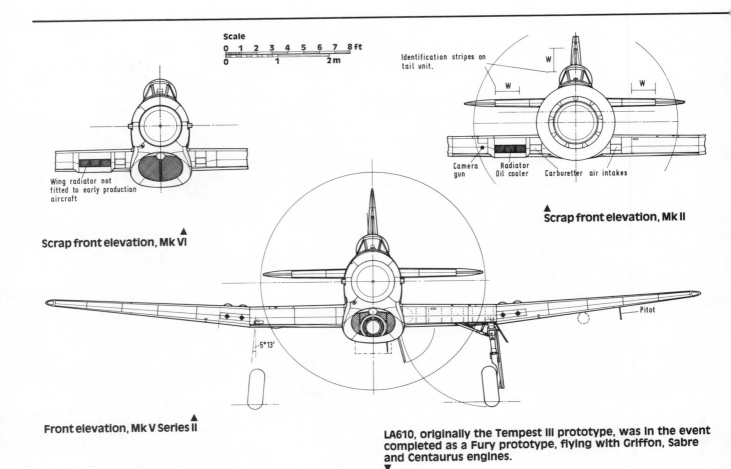

Scale

0 1 2 3 4 5 6 7 8 ft

0   1   2 m

Identification stripes on tail unit.

W

W   W

Camera gun   Radiator Oil cooler   Carburetter air intakes

▲ **Scrap front elevation, Mk II**

Wing radiator not fitted to early production aircraft

▲

Scrap front elevation, Mk VI

Pitot

5° 13'

Front elevation, Mk V Series II ▲

LA610, originally the Tempest III prototype, was in the event completed as a Fury prototype, flying with Griffon, Sabre and Centaurus engines.
▼

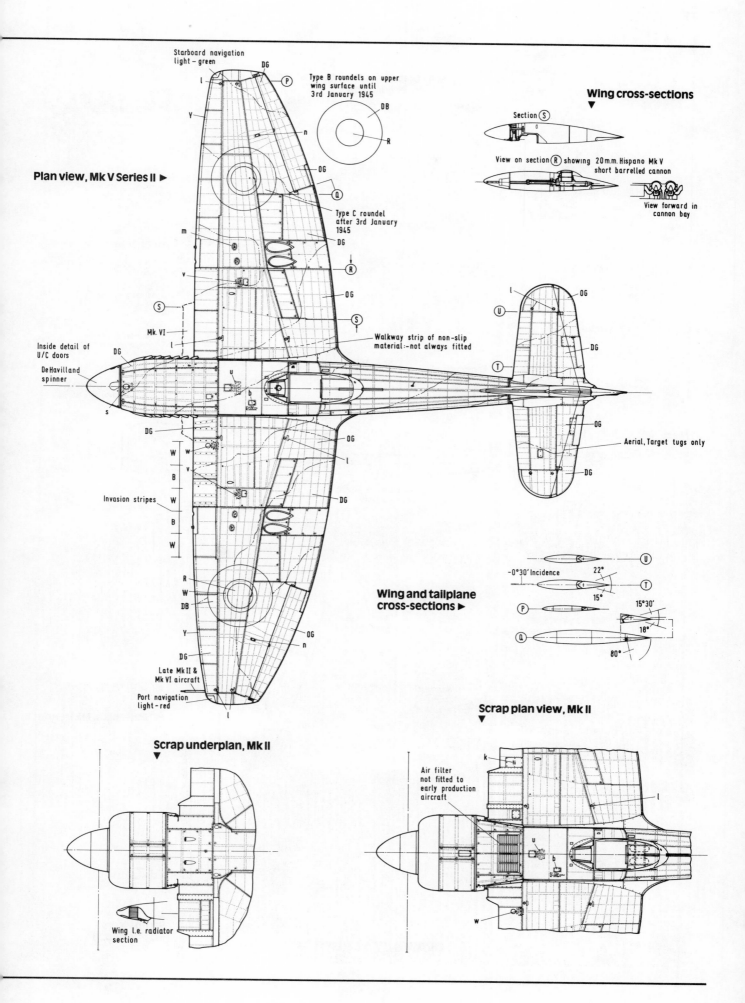

Plan view, Mk V Series II ▶

Starboard navigation
light – green

Type B roundels on upper
wing surface until
3rd January 1945

DB

R

Type C roundel
after 3rd January
1945

Wing cross-sections
▼

Section S

View on section R showing 20 m.m. Hispano Mk V
short barrelled cannon

View forward in
cannon bay

Inside detail of
U/C doors

De Havilland
spinner

Mk. VI

Walkway strip of non-slip
material :- not always fitted

Aerial, Target tugs only

Invasion stripes

Late Mk II &
Mk VI aircraft

Port navigation
light – red

Wing and tailplane
cross-sections ▶

-0°30' Incidence   22°

15°

15°30'

18°

80°

Scrap plan view, Mk II
▼

Air filter
not fitted to
early production
aircraft

Scrap underplan, Mk II
▼

Wing l.e. radiator
section

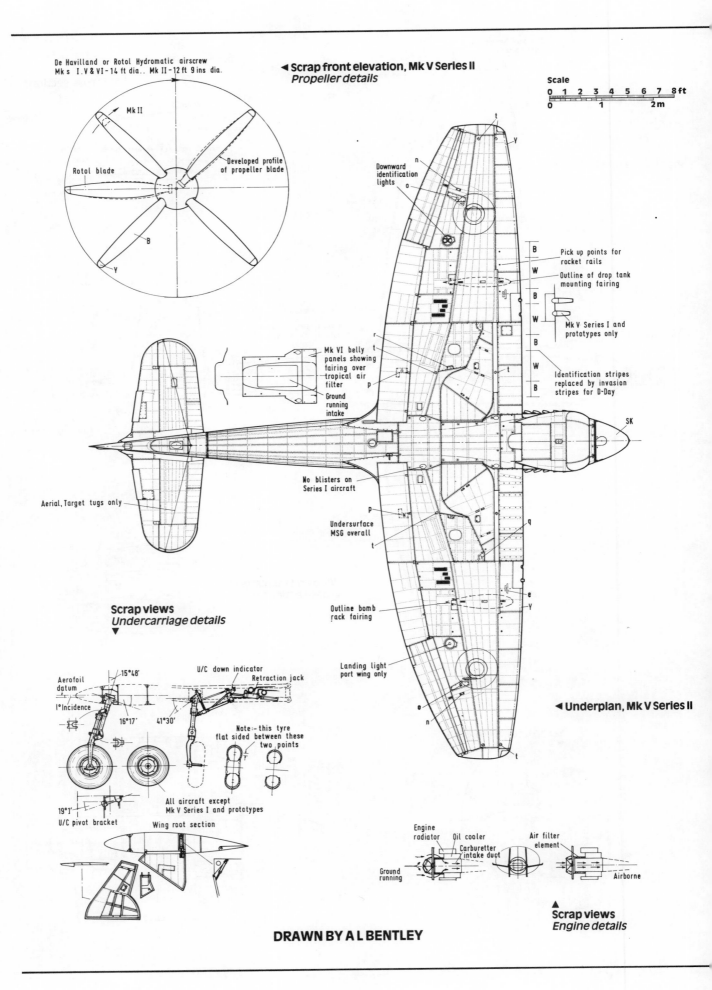

De Havilland or Rotol Hydromatic airscrew
Mks I. V & VI-14 ft dia.. Mk II-12 ft 9 ins dia.

Mk II

Rotol blade

Developed profile
of propeller blade

B

Y

◀ **Scrap front elevation, Mk V Series II**
Propeller details

Downward
identification
lights

n

o

t

Y

B
W
B
W
B
W
B

Pick up points for
rocket rails

Outline of drop tank
mounting fairing

Mk V Series I and
prototypes only

Identification stripes
replaced by invasion
stripes for D-Day

r

t

Mk VI belly
panels showing
fairing over
tropical air
filter

p

Ground
running
intake

No blisters on
Series I aircraft

Aerial, Target tugs only

p

Undersurface
MSG overall

t

q

e

Y

SK

Outline bomb
rack fairing

Landing light
port wing only

o

n

t

◀ **Underplan, Mk V Series II**

Scrap views
Undercarriage details
▼

Aerofoil
datum

15°48'

U/C down indicator

Retraction jack

1° Incidence

16°17'

41°30'

Note:- this tyre
flat sided between these
two points

19°1'

U/C pivot bracket

All aircraft except
Mk V Series I and prototypes

Wing root section

Engine
radiator   Oil cooler

Carburetter
intake duct

Air filter
element

Ground
running

Airborne

▲
Scrap views
Engine details

DRAWN BY A L BENTLEY

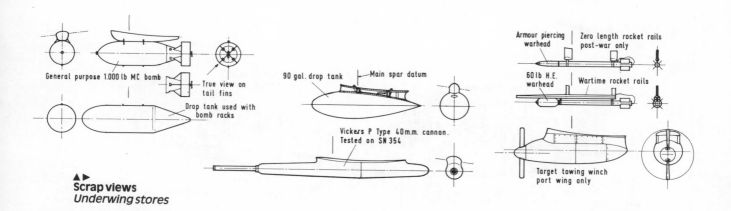

General purpose 1,000 lb MC bomb

True view on tail fins

Drop tank used with bomb racks

90 gal. drop tank — Main spar datum

Vickers P Type 40 m.m. cannon. Tested on SN 354

Armour piercing warhead | Zero length rocket rails post-war only

60 lb H.E. warhead | Wartime rocket rails

Target towing winch port wing only

▲▶ Scrap views
Underwing stores

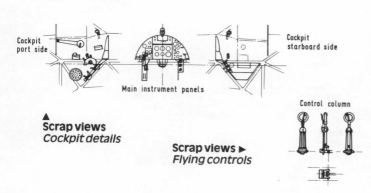

Cockpit port side

Main instrument panels

Cockpit starboard side

▲ Scrap views
Cockpit details

Scrap views ▶
Flying controls

Control column

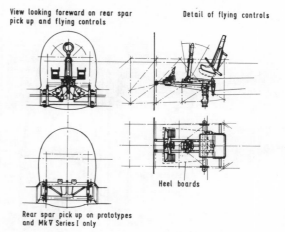

View looking foreward on rear spar pick up and flying controls

Detail of flying controls

Heel boards

Rear spar pick up on prototypes and Mk V Series I only

Tempest V Series II, now at the RAF Museum. These big, powerful fighters showed considerable performance improvements over the aerodynamically inferior Typhoons.
▼

NV778

Scale

0 1 2 3 4 5 6 7 8 ft

0   1   2 m

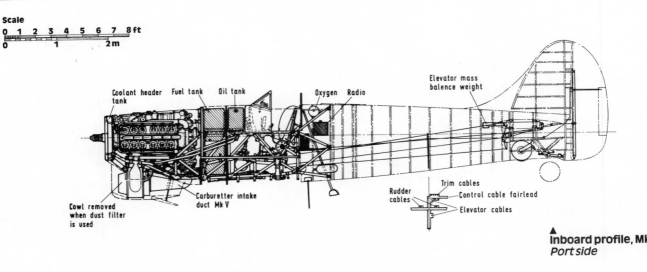

Coolant header tank

Fuel tank

Oil tank

Oxygen

Radio

Elevator mass balence weight

Cowl removed when dust filter is used

Carburetter intake duct Mk V

Trim cables

Rudder cables

Control cable fairlead

Elevator cables

▲ **Inboard profile, Mk V**
Port side

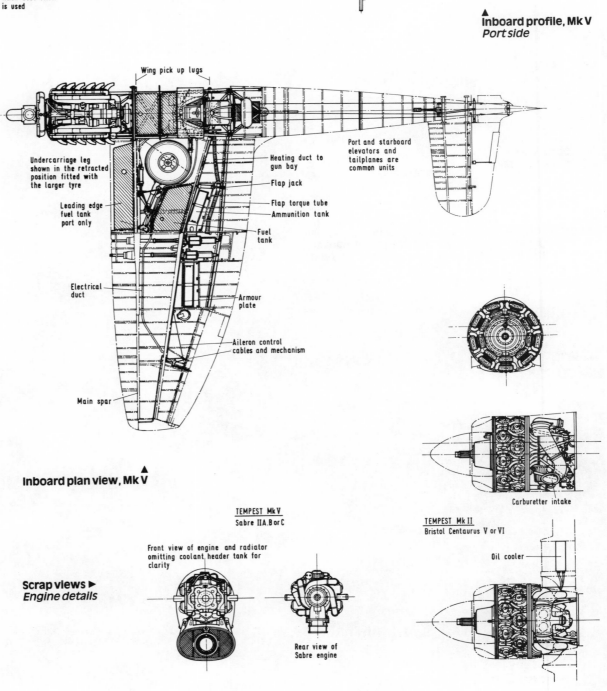

Wing pick up lugs

Undercarriage leg shown in the retracted position fitted with the larger tyre

Leading edge fuel tank port only

Electrical duct

Main spar

Heating duct to gun bay

Flap jack

Flap torque tube

Ammunition tank

Fuel tank

Armour plate

Aileron control cables and mechanism

Port and starboard elevators and tailplanes are common units

Inboard plan view, Mk V ▲

Carburetter intake

TEMPEST Mk V
Sabre IIA.B or C

Front view of engine and radiator omitting coolant header tank for clarity

Rear view of Sabre engine

Scrap views ▶
Engine details

TEMPEST Mk II
Bristol Centaurus V or VI

Oil cooler

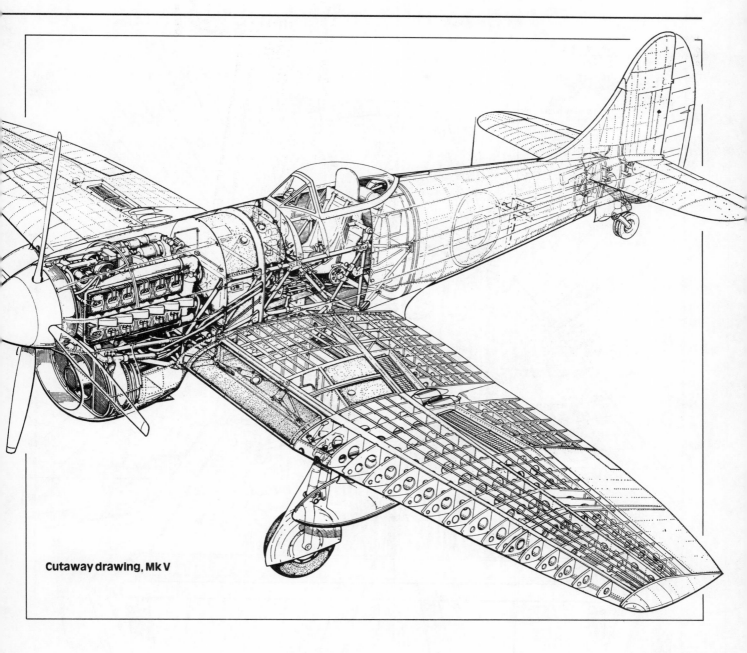

Cutaway drawing, Mk V

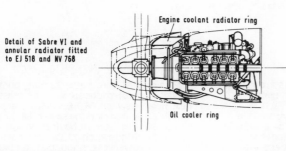

Detail of Sabre VI and annular radiator fitted to EJ 518 and NV 768

Engine coolant radiator ring

Oil cooler ring

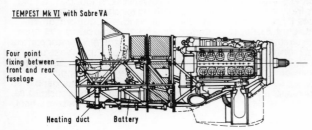

TEMPEST Mk VI with Sabre VA

Four point fixing between front and rear fuselage

Heating duct   Battery

Gunsight :- early Mk.V only.

Gunsight :- Mk.II & Mk.V.

Gunsight :- Mk.VI & late Mk.II only.

▲ **Scrap views**
Gun sights

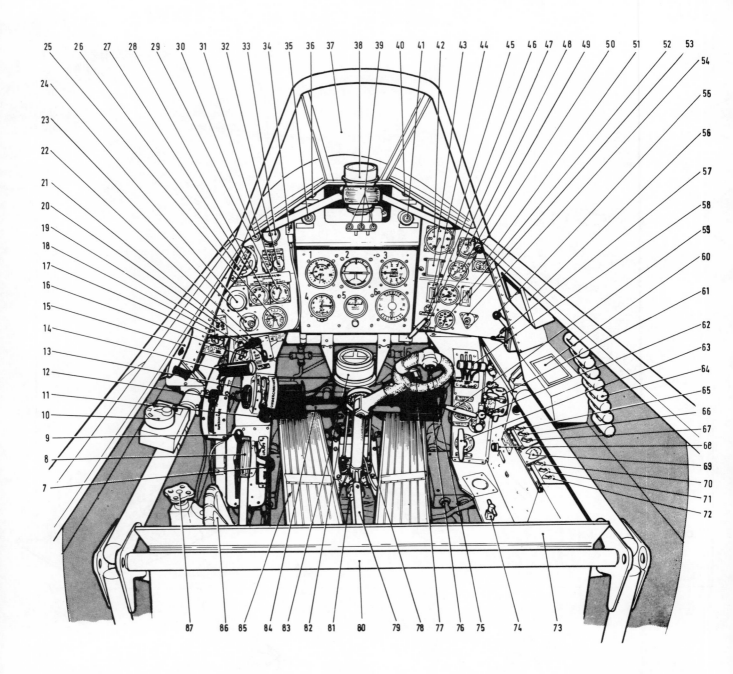

Numerical key

1. Airspeed indicator. 2. Artificial horizon. 3. Rate of climb indicator. 4. Altimeter. 5. Direction indicator. 6. Turn and bank indicator. 7. Flap lever. 8. Hydraulic hand pump. 9. Radiator shutter lever. 10. Gunsight control weapons selector box. 11. Undercarriage lever. 12. Supercharger lever. 13. Throttle friction knob. 14. Throttle lever. 15. Canopy winding handle. 16. Reading lamp switch. 17. Undercarriage emergency release switch. 18. Undercarriage indicator lights. 19. Beam approach button. 20. Magnetic switches. 21. Cut-out safety control. 22. Propeller pitch lever. 23. Punkah louvres (late models only). 24. Watch holder. 25. Wheel brake pressure indicators. 26. T.R. 1143 control unit. 27. Undercarriage indicators. 28. Oxygen delivery indicator. 29. Oxygen supply indicator. 30. Contactor switch. 31. Engine starting, boost

coil switch. 32. Engine starting starter switch. 33. Remote contactor. 34. Flap position indicator. 35. Reflector sight switch. 36. Cockpit light switch (port). 37. Armoured windscreen. 38. Gunsight. 39. Spare bulbs for gunsight. 40. Cockpit light switch (starboard). 41. Compass light switch. 42. Rev counter. 43. Compass card. 44. Oil pressure indicator. 45. Fuel pressure indicator light. 46. Hood jettison lever. 47. Power failure warning light. 48. Boost gauge. 49. Fuel contents (main tank). 50. Oil temperature indicator. 51. Fuel contents (wing tanks). 52. Radiator temperature indicator. 53. Fuel pressure gauge. 54. Punkah louvre (late models). 55. Cockpit heating lever. 56. Very pistol opening. 57. Fuel tank pressure lever. 58. Fuel cocks (inter, main and nose tanks). 59. Cylinder priming pump. 60. Engine data card. 61. Signalling switch box. 62. Windscreen anti-

icing pumps. 63. Carburettor priming pump. 64. Very pistol cartridge stowage. 65. Pressure head heating switch. 66. T.R. 1143 master switch. 67. Heated clothing switch. 68. Dimmer switch. 69. Voltmeter. 70. Navigation light switch. 71. Rising switch. 72. Camera master switch. 73. Lower seat armour plate (upper armour omitted for clarity). 74. Cartridge starter reload handle. 75. Gun button. 76. Control column. 77. Radio button. 78. Push rods for aileron control. 79. Elevator control push rod. 80. Basic front fuselage structure of tubular steel. 81. Universal joint, aileron torque tube. 82. Handwheel for rudder bar adjustment. 83. Compass. 84. Rudder bar. 85. Heel boards (no floor as such to cockpit). 86. Elevator trim wheel. 87. Rudder trim wheel.

Northrop P-61A and B Black Widow

Country of origin: USA.
Type: Two- or (B) three-seat, land-based night fighter.
Dimensions: Wing span 66ft 0in *20.12m*; length 48ft 11in *14.91m*; height 14ft 2in *4.32m*; wing area 664 sq ft *61.69m²*.
Weights: Empty 20,965lb *9512kg*, (B) 21,282lb *9656kg*; normal loaded 27,600lb *12,523kg*, (B) 29,700lb *13,475kg*; maximum

32,400lb *14,700kg*, (B) 38,000lb *17,241kg*.
Powerplant: Two Pratt & Whitney R2800-65 Double Wasp eighteen-cylinder radial engines each rated at 2250hp.
Performance: Maximum speed 369mph *520kph* at 20,000ft *6100m*, (B) 366mph *516kph* at 20,000ft; time to 5000ft *1525m*, 2.2min, (B) 2.7min; service ceiling 33,000ft *10,060m*; range (clean) 1010 miles

1626km, (B) 940 miles *1515km*.
Armament: Four fixed 20mm cannon and (some aircraft) four barbette-mounted 0.5in machine guns, plus two 1000lb *454kg* or 1600lb *726kg* bombs or (B) four 1000lb or 1600lb bombs.
Service: First flight (XP-61) 21 May 1942; service entry (P-61A) October 1943, (B) summer 1944.

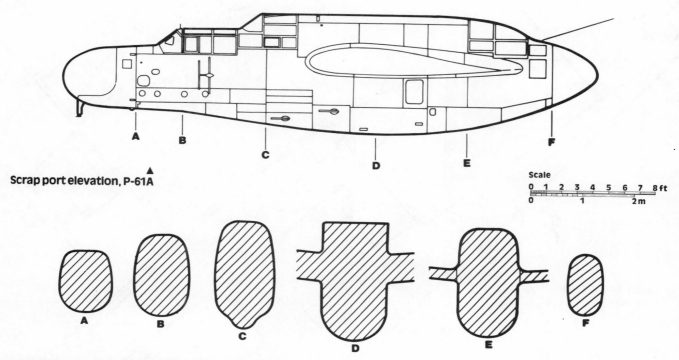

▲
Scrap port elevation, P-61A

Scale

The P-61 Black Widow was the first US aircraft designed specifically for the night fighting role.
▼

▲
Fuselage cross-sections

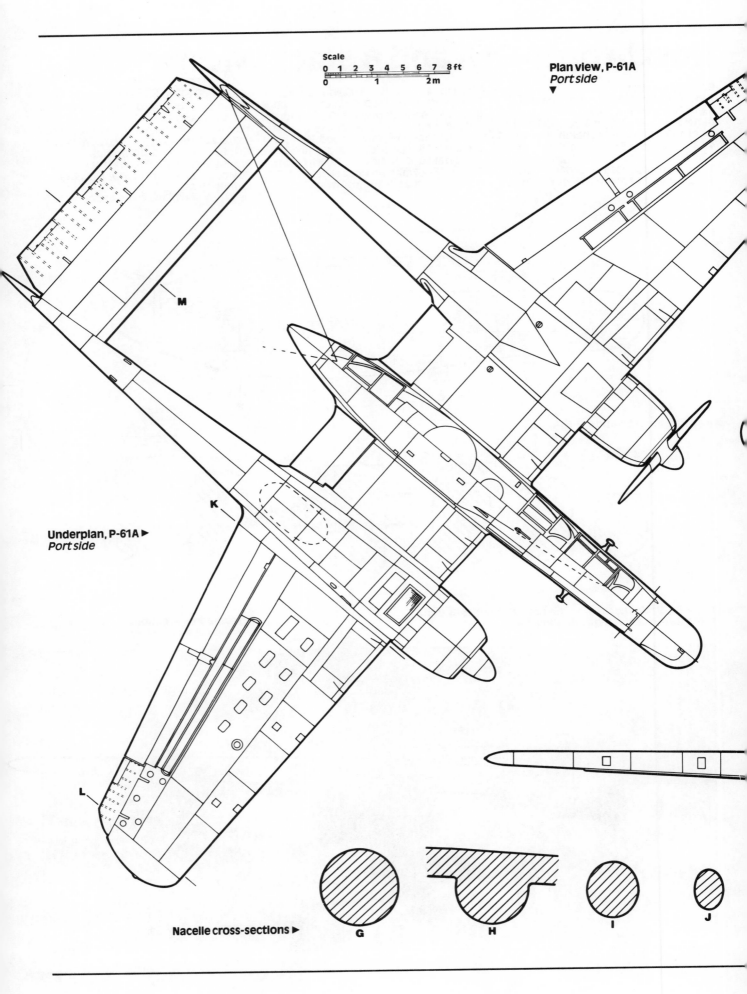

Scale

0 1 2 3 4 5 6 7 8 ft

0   1   2 m

Plan view, P-61A
Port side
▼

M

K

Underplan, P-61A ▶
Port side

L

Nacelle cross-sections ▶

G   H   I   J

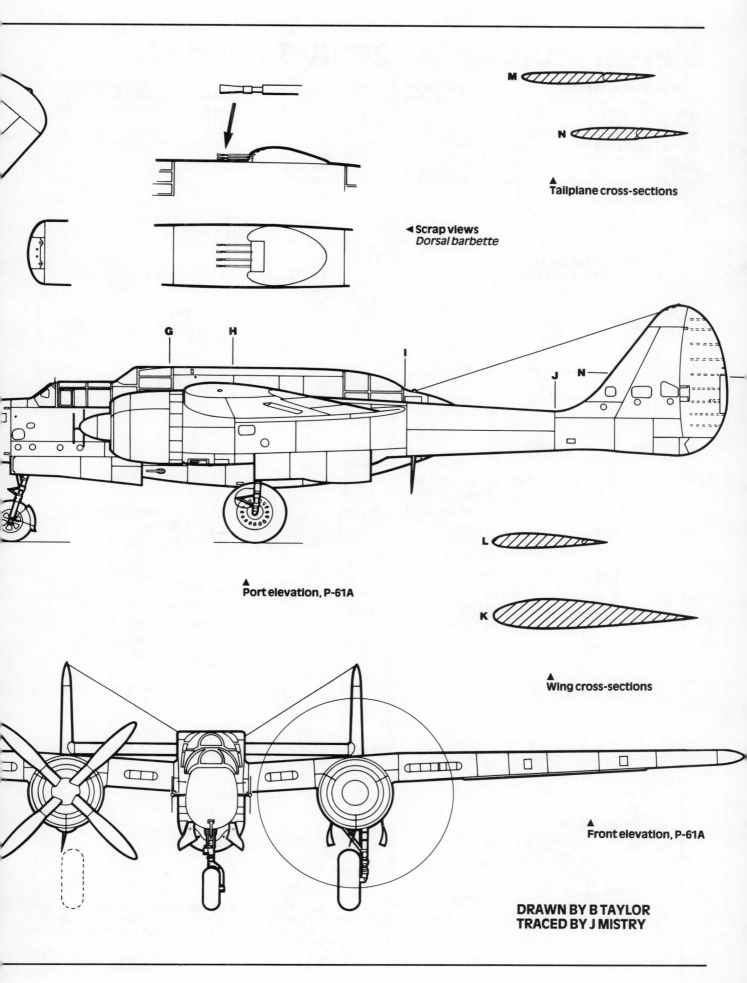

M

N

▲ Tailplane cross-sections

◀ Scrap views
Dorsal barbette

G   H   I

J   N

▲ Port elevation, P-61A

L

K

▲ Wing cross-sections

▲ Front elevation, P-61A

**DRAWN BY B TAYLOR
TRACED BY J MISTRY**

Messerschmitt Me 262A-1a and -2a

Country of origin: Germany.
Type: Single-seat, land-based interceptor fighter or (A-2a) fighter bomber.
Dimensions: Wing span 40ft 11½in *12.48m*; length 34ft 9½in *10.60m*; height 12ft 7in *3.84m*; wing area 234 sq ft *21.74m²*.
Weights: Empty 8375lb *3800kg*; empty

equipped 9742lb *4420kg*; loaded 14,106lb *6400kg*; maximum 15,720lb *7132kg*.
Powerplant: Two Junkers Jumo 004B-1, -2 or -3 axial-flow turbojets each of 1980lb *989kg* static thrust.
Performance: Maximum speed 540mph *870kph* at 19,685ft *6000m*; initial climb rate 3935ft/min *1200m/min*; service ceiling 37,565ft *11,450m*; range (clean)

652 miles *1050km* at 29,525ft *9000m*.
Armament: Four fixed 30mm MK 108 cannon, plus (A-2a) two 551lb *250kg* bombs.
Service: First flight (turbojet Me 262V-1) 18 July 1942; service entry (A-1a) July 1944.

DRAWN BY IAN R STAIR
TRACED BY A A P LLOYD

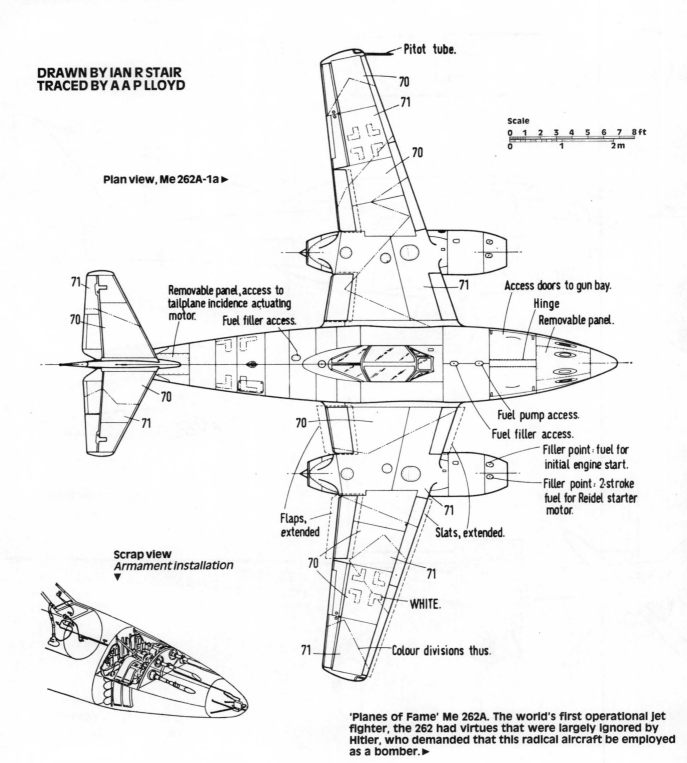

Pitot tube.

70
71
70

Scale
0 1 2 3 4 5 6 7 8ft
0 1 2m

Plan view, Me 262A-1a ▶

71

Access doors to gun bay.

Hinge
Removable panel.

71

Removable panel, access to tailplane incidence actuating motor.
Fuel filler access.

70

71

70

70

71

Fuel pump access.
Fuel filler access.

Filler point: fuel for initial engine start.

Filler point: 2-stroke fuel for Reidel starter motor.

Flaps, extended

70

71

Slats, extended.

Scrap view
Armament installation
▼

WHITE.

71

Colour divisions thus.

'Planes of Fame' Me 262A. The world's first operational jet fighter, the 262 had virtues that were largely ignored by Hitler, who demanded that this radical aircraft be employed as a bomber. ▶

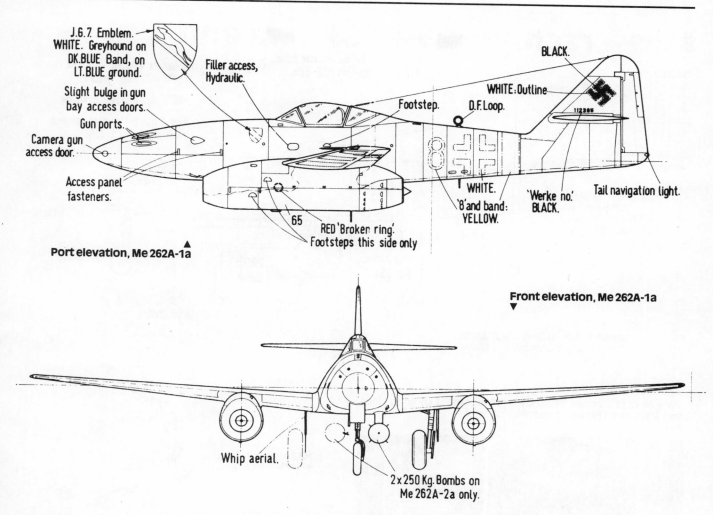

J.6.7. Emblem. WHITE. Greyhound on DK.BLUE Band, on LT.BLUE ground.

Slight bulge in gun bay access doors.

Gun ports.

Camera gun access door.

Access panel fasteners.

Filler access, Hydraulic.

Footstep.

D.F. Loop.

BLACK.

WHITE: Outline

112305

WHITE. '8' and band: YELLOW.

'Werke no.' BLACK.

Tail navigation light.

65

RED 'Broken ring'. Footsteps this side only

Port elevation, Me 262A-1a ▲

Front elevation, Me 262A-1a ▼

Whip aerial.

2 x 250 Kg. Bombs on Me 262A-2a only.

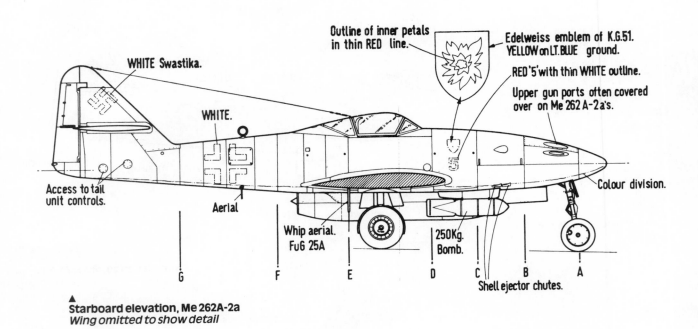

Outline of inner petals in thin RED line.

Edelweiss emblem of K.G.51. YELLOW on LT.BLUE ground.

WHITE Swastika.

RED '5' with thin WHITE outline.

WHITE.

Upper gun ports often covered over on Me 262 A-2a's.

Access to tail unit controls.

Aerial

Whip aerial. FuG 25A

250Kg. Bomb.

Colour division.

Shell ejector chutes.

G   F   E   D   C   B   A

▲ **Starboard elevation, Me 262A-2a**
Wing omitted to show detail

View of captured Me 262 shows arrangement of wing flaps and slats and sideways-opening canopy.
▼

Czech-built Me 262A-1 preserved at Prague's Technical Museum, in overall glossy grey finish.
▼

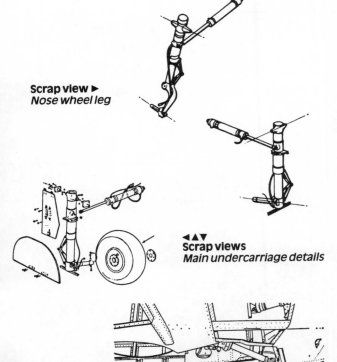

Scrap view ▶
Nose wheel leg

◀▲▼
Scrap views
Main undercarriage details

▲
Scrap view
Tyre tread pattern

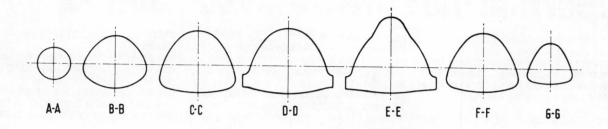

A-A B-B C-C D-D E-E F-F G-G

Fuselage cross-sections ▲

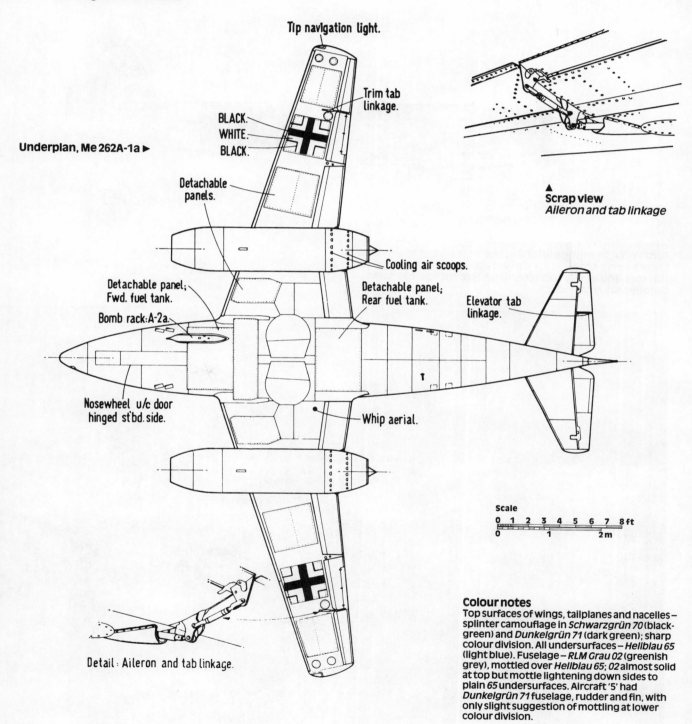

Tip navigation light.

Trim tab linkage.

BLACK.
WHITE.
BLACK.

Underplan, Me 262A-1a ▶

Detachable panels.

Detachable panel; Fwd. fuel tank.

Bomb rack: A-2a.

Nosewheel u/c door hinged st'bd. side.

Cooling air scoops.

Detachable panel; Rear fuel tank.

Elevator tab linkage.

Whip aerial.

Scrap view
Aileron and tab linkage

Detail : Aileron and tab linkage.

Scale
0 1 2 3 4 5 6 7 8 ft
0   1   2 m

Colour notes
Top surfaces of wings, tailplanes and nacelles – splinter camouflage in *Schwarzgrün 70* (black-green) and *Dunkelgrün 71* (dark green); sharp colour division. All undersurfaces – *Hellblau 65* (light blue). Fuselage – *RLM Grau 02* (greenish grey), mottled over *Hellblau 65*; *02* almost solid at top but mottle lightening down sides to plain *65* undersurfaces. Aircraft '5' had *Dunkelgrün 71* fuselage, rudder and fin, with only slight suggestion of mottling at lower colour division.

Supermarine Spitfire Mks 21 and 22

Country of origin: Great Britain.
Type: Single-seat, land-based interceptor fighter and fighter-bomber.
Dimensions: Wing span 36ft 11in *11.25m;* length 32ft 8in *9.96m;* height (maximum) 13ft 6in *4.11m;* wing area 244 sq ft *22.67m².*
Weights: Empty 6900lb *3131kg;*

maximum 9200lb *4174kg.*
Powerplant: One Rolls-Royce Griffon 61 or 64 V12, liquid-cooled piston engine rated at 2050hp, (Mk 22) Griffon 61, 64 or 85 rated at 2050hp.
Performance: Maximum speed 454mph *731kph* at 26,000ft *7925m;* time to 20,000ft *6100m,* 8min; service ceiling

43,500ft *13,260m;* range (clean) 490 miles *789km.*
Armament: Four fixed 20mm Hispano cannon plus (optional) one 500lb *227kg* and two 250lb *113kg* bombs
Service: First flight (prototype Mk 21) 24 July 1943, (production Mk 21) 15 March 1944; service entry (Mk 21) January 1945.

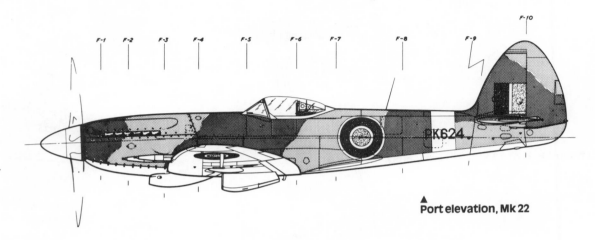

▲ **Port elevation, Mk 22**

Spitfire Mk 21 represented a major redesign of the familiar Supermarine shape, with a new type of wing, enlarged tail surfaces and a fully retractable undercarriage. Old-style canopy was retained.
▼

CAMOUFLAGE COLOURS
DARK SEA GREEN
CAMOUFLAGE BROWN
UNDERSIDE: SKY BLUE

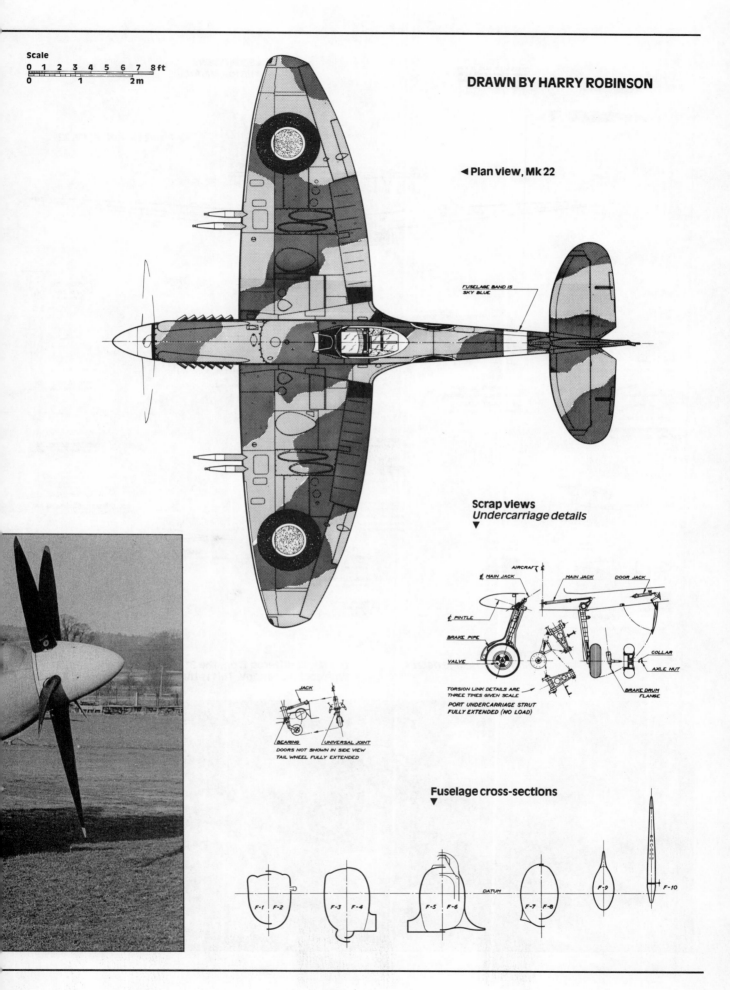

Scale

0 1 2 3 4 5 6 7 8 ft

0　　　1　　　2 m

DRAWN BY HARRY ROBINSON

◄ **Plan view, Mk 22**

FUSELAGE BAND IS
SKY BLUE

Scrap views
Undercarriage details
▼

AIRCRAFT ₵

₵ MAIN JACK　　　MAIN JACK　　　DOOR JACK

₵ PINTLE

BRAKE PIPE

VALVE

COLLAR

AXLE NUT

BRAKE DRUM
FLANGE

TORSION LINK DETAILS ARE
THREE TIMES GIVEN SCALE

PORT UNDERCARRIAGE STRUT
FULLY EXTENDED (NO LOAD)

JACK

BEARING　　UNIVERSAL JOINT

DOORS NOT SHOWN IN SIDE VIEW
TAIL WHEEL FULLY EXTENDED

Fuselage cross-sections
▼

DATUM

F-1　F-2　　　F-3　F-4　　　F-5　F-6　　　F-7　F-8　　F-9　　F-10

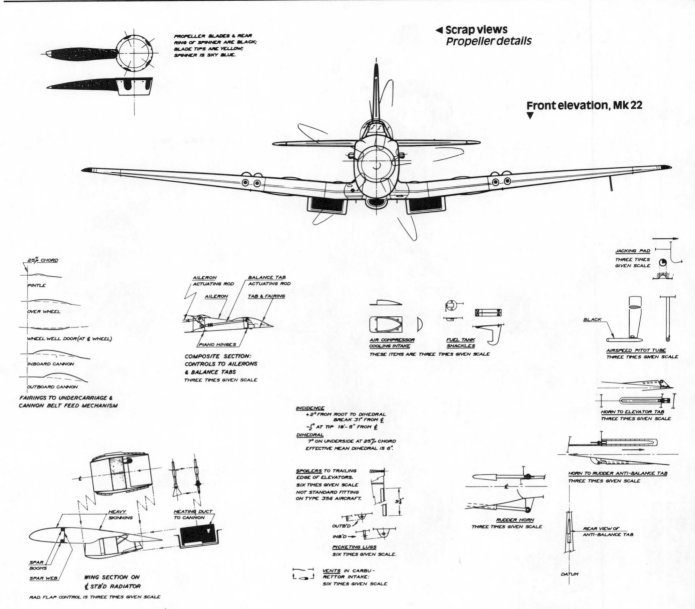

PROPELLER BLADES & REAR
RING OF SPINNER ARE BLACK;
BLADE TIPS ARE YELLOW;
SPINNER IS SKY BLUE.

◀ **Scrap views**
Propeller details

Front elevation, Mk 22
▼

25% CHORD

PINTLE

OVER WHEEL

WHEEL WELL DOOR (AT ℄ WHEEL)

INBOARD CANNON

OUTBOARD CANNON

FAIRINGS TO UNDERCARRIAGE &
CANNON BELT FEED MECHANISM

AILERON
ACTUATING ROD

BALANCE TAB
ACTUATING ROD

AILERON

TAB & FAIRING

PIANO HINGES

COMPOSITE SECTION:
CONTROLS TO AILERONS
& BALANCE TABS
THREE TIMES GIVEN SCALE

AIR COMPRESSOR
COOLING INTAKE
THESE ITEMS ARE THREE TIMES GIVEN SCALE

FUEL TANK
SHACKLES

JACKING PAD
THREE TIMES
GIVEN SCALE

BLACK

AIRSPEED PITOT TUBE
THREE TIMES GIVEN SCALE

INCIDENCE
+2° FROM ROOT TO DIHEDRAL
BREAK 31" FROM ℄
–½° AT TIP 18'-5" FROM ℄

DIHEDRAL
7° ON UNDERSIDE AT 25% CHORD
EFFECTIVE MEAN DIHEDRAL IS 6°.

SPOILERS TO TRAILING
EDGE OF ELEVATORS.
SIX TIMES GIVEN SCALE
NOT STANDARD FITTING
ON TYPE 356 AIRCRAFT.

HORN TO ELEVATOR TAB
THREE TIMES GIVEN SCALE

HORN TO RUDDER ANTI-BALANCE TAB
THREE TIMES GIVEN SCALE

OUTB'D

INB'D

PICKETING LUGS
SIX TIMES GIVEN SCALE.

RUDDER HORN
THREE TIMES GIVEN SCALE

REAR VIEW OF
ANTI-BALANCE TAB

DATUM

HEAVY
SKINNING

HEATING DUCT
TO CANNON

SPAR
BOOMS

SPAR WEB

WING SECTION ON
℄ STB'D RADIATOR

RAD. FLAP CONTROL IS THREE TIMES GIVEN SCALE

VENTS IN CARBU-
RETTOR INTAKE:
SIX TIMES GIVEN SCALE

▲ **Scrap views**
Wing and fuselage details

**The Mk 22 differed from the 21 mainly in having a 'bubble'
type cockpit canopy. This is the first production aircraft.**
▼

▲
Both the Mk 21 and 22 were too late to see combat in WW2, and most of the 400 or so aircraft produced went to RAF auxiliary squadrons.

Underplan, Mk 22 ▶

Scale

```
0  1  2  3  4  5  6  7  8 ft
0              1          2 m
```

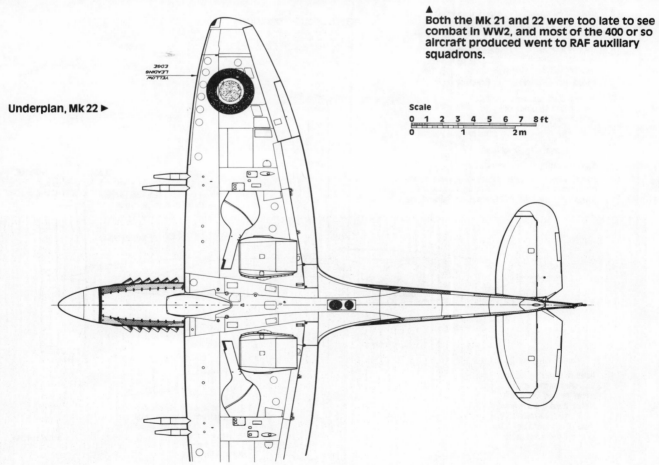

YELLOW LEADING EDGE

Heinkel He 162A-2 Salamander

Country of origin: Germany.
Type: Single-seat, land based interceptor fighter.
Dimensions: Wing span 23ft 7½in *7.20m*; length 29ft 8¼in *9.05m*; height 8ft 6¼in *2.60m*; wing area 120.56 sq ft *11.20m²*.
Weights: Empty 3666lb *1663kg*; empty equipped 3875lb *1758kg*; normal loaded

5744lb *2606kg*; maximum loaded 6184lb *2806kg*.
Powerplant: One BMW 003E-1 or -2 axial-flow turbojet of 1764lb *800kg* static thrust.
Performance: Maximum speed 562mph *905kph* at 19,690ft *6000m*; initial climb rate (maximum thrust) 4615ft/min

1405m/min; service ceiling 39,400ft *12,000m*; range (maximum) 587 miles *945km*.
Armament: Two fixed 20mm MG 151 cannon.
Service: First flight (He 162V-1) 6 December 1944, (A-2) 24 January 1945; service entry February 1945.

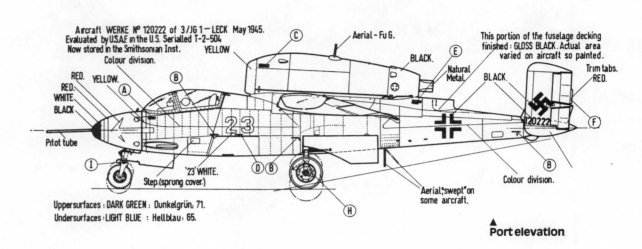

Aircraft WERKE № 120222 of 3/JG 1 – LECK May 1945.
Evaluated by U.S.A.F in the U.S. Serialled T-2-504
Now stored in the Smithsonian Inst.
Colour division.

Uppersurfaces : DARK GREEN : Dunkelgrün: 71.
Undersurfaces : LIGHT BLUE : Hellblau: 65.

▲ Port elevation

	Aubenbordsteckdose im Bugrädraum.	Electrical socket in nosewheel well.
Ⓐ		
Ⓑ	Hier Unterbocken.	Under supports (trestles) here.
Ⓒ	Vor dem offen der Spannverschlüsse oben Verschlüssel links u rechts offen.	Before opening the catches above open latches left and right.
Ⓓ	Sauerstoff Anschluss.	Oxygen connection.
Ⓔ	Vor dem Start muss startmannshaft Kortrallieren ob Düse auf S-Stellung gehfaren l.	Before the start the starting crew must check that the nozzle has gone into the S-position.
Ⓕ	Nicht Anfassen.	Do not touch.
Ⓖ	Nicht Betreten.	Do not walk here.
Ⓗ	Achtung: Räder nicht temlem beror reifen lufleer.	Caution: Do not split the rims before deflating the tyres.
Ⓘ	Reifen Fulldruck 3 atü.	Tyre pressure 3 atmospheres.

◄ Stencilled instructions

Scale
0 1 2 3 4 5 6 7 8ft
0 1 2m

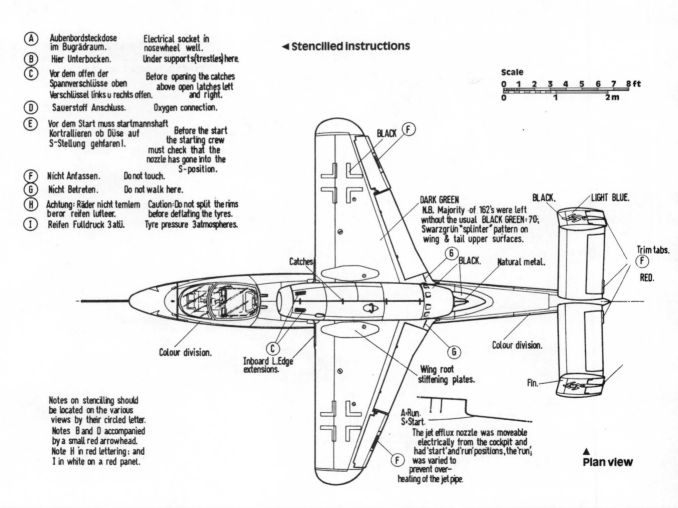

DARK GREEN
N.B. Majority of 162's were left without the usual BLACK GREEN: 70; Swarzgrün "splinter" pattern on wing & tail upper surfaces.

A=Run.
S=Start.
The jet efflux nozzle was moveable electrically from the cockpit and had 'start' and 'run' positions, the 'run' was varied to prevent over-heating of the jet pipe.

▲ Plan view

Notes on stencilling should be located on the various views by their circled letter. Notes B and D accompanied by a small red arrowhead. Note H in red lettering; and I in white on a red panel.

▲ Imperial War Museum's He 162, Wk Nr
120235, finished in JG 77 scheme.

Motor cowl
rests on wing
when 'open'.

55° Anhedral
Wing tips.

Brakes on Mainwheels
only; Non-steerable
Nosewheel.

▲
Front elevation

Scrap port elevation ▶
Sectioned nose of powerplant

Nose fairing.

Oil tank.

Starting fuel
tank.

Bullet
fairing.

Reidel
starter.

Intake.

Manual
pull ring.

Clutch.

By-pass.

Oil cooler.

Pair of exhausts.

DRAWN BY A A P LLOYD

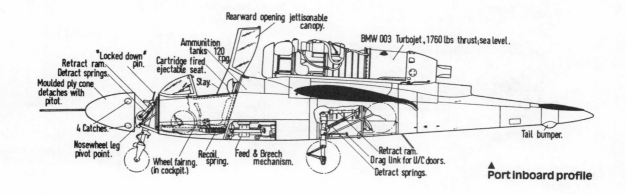

Rearward opening jettisonable
canopy.

Ammunition
tanks 120
rpg.

BMW 003 Turbojet, 1760 lbs thrust; sea level.

"Locked down"
pin.

Retract ram.

Detract springs.

Cartridge fired
ejectable seat.

Stay.

Moulded ply cone
detaches with
pitot.

4 Catches.

Nosewheel leg
pivot point.

Wheel fairing.
(in cockpit.)

Recoil
spring.

Feed & Breech
mechanism.

Retract ram.

Drag link for U/C doors.

Detract springs.

Tail bumper.

▲
Port inboard profile

He 162 Wk Nr 120076 housed in the Rockliffe Museum in Ottawa was operational with 1/JG 1 at the close of the war. Like many other radical German designs, the 'People's Fighter' came too late to affect the outcome of the conflict.

Wing cross-sections
▼

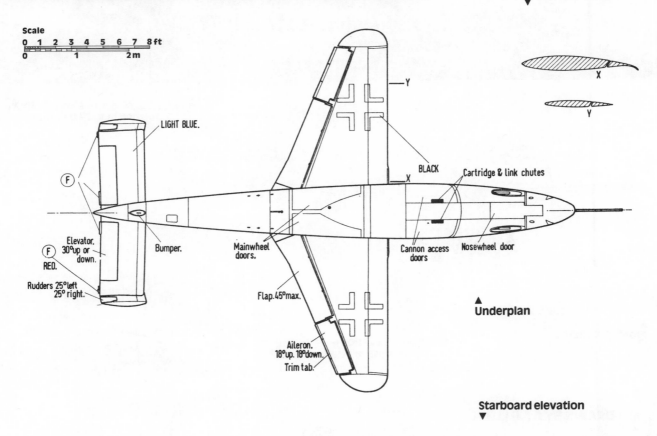

LIGHT BLUE.

F

Elevator. 30°up or down.

F

RED.

Rudders 25°left 25° right.

Bumper.

Mainwheel doors.

Flap. 45°max.

Aileron. 18°up. 18°down.

Trim tab.

BLACK

X

Cartridge & link chutes

Cannon access doors

Nosewheel door

▲ **Underplan**

Starboard elevation
▼

Aircraft WERKE N° 120076 Formerly of 1/JG 1 – LECK May 1945. Now re-finished as aircraft '4'. of 9/JG 77. In the Canadian War Museum, ROCKLIFFE.

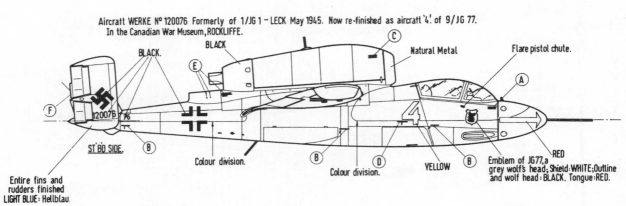

BLACK.

BLACK

E

C

Natural Metal

Flare pistol chute.

A

F

120076

Colour division.

B

Colour division.

B

D

YELLOW

B

RED

ST BD SIDE.

Entire fins and rudders finished LIGHT BLUE: Hellblau.

Emblem of JG77,a grey wolf's head; Shield:WHITE;Outline and wolf head:BLACK. Tongue:RED.

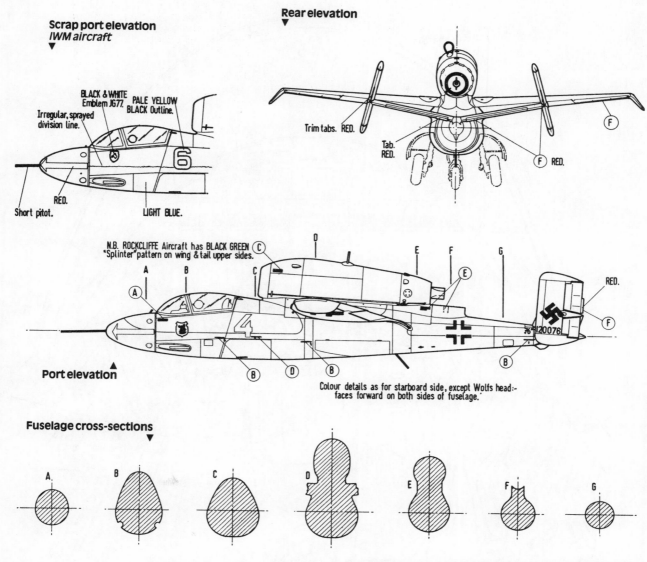

Scrap port elevation
IWM aircraft
▼

Irregular, sprayed division line.

BLACK & WHITE Emblem JG77.

PALE YELLOW BLACK Outline.

Short pitot.

RED.

LIGHT BLUE.

Rear elevation
▼

Trim tabs. RED.

Tab. RED.

F RED.

F

N.B. ROCKCLIFFE Aircraft has BLACK GREEN © "Splinter" pattern on wing & tail upper sides.

A B C D E F G

RED.

120076

F

Port elevation
▲

Colour details as for starboard side, except Wolfs head:-
faces forward on both sides of fuselage.

Fuselage cross-sections
▼

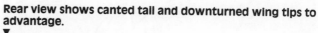

A B C D E F G

Rear view shows canted tail and downturned wing tips to advantage.
▼

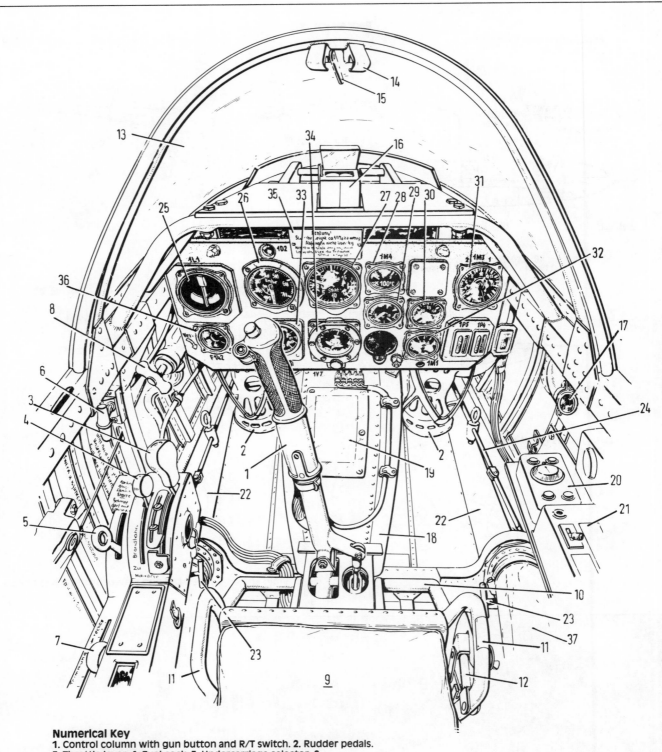

Numerical Key

1. Control column with gun button and R/T switch. 2. Rudder pedals.
3. Throttle lever. 4. Fuel cock. 5. Undercarriage selector. 6.
Undercarriage operating lever. 7. Trimming control. 8. Flap control. 9.
Ejection seat. 10. Foot stirrups. 11. Seat handles. 12. Starboard handle
with ejection trigger. 13. Front canopy. 14. Canopy catch. 15. Canopy
release. 16. Revi gunsight. 17. Flare pistol chute. 18. Nosewheel cover.
19. Window for visual check. 20. Radio selector. 21. Starter and
electrical panel. 22. Cannon blast tubes. 23. Cannon forward mount.
24. Manual cocking levers. 25. Turn and bank. 26. Airspeed indicator. 27.
Rate of climb/descent. 28. Jet pipe temperature. 29. Pressure gauge
(red rim). 30. Pressure gauge (yellow rim). 31. RPM. 32. Fuel contents
gauge (yellow rim). 33. Altimeter. 34. Compass. 35. Limit data. 36. Flap
indicator. 37. Canvas recoil spring covers.

"LIMIT" Plate 35

See cockpit drawing.

Achtung!
Stauröhr zeigt ca 10% zu wenig
Abfangen nicht über 4g
Negativ beschleunigung nicht läng als
3 sek du Tritwerk sonst ausgeht.·

Equivalent:
Caution! Pitot tube shows 10% to little : Do not flatten out
above 4g : Do not use negative acceleration more than 3secs
otherwise the turbine shaft will fail.

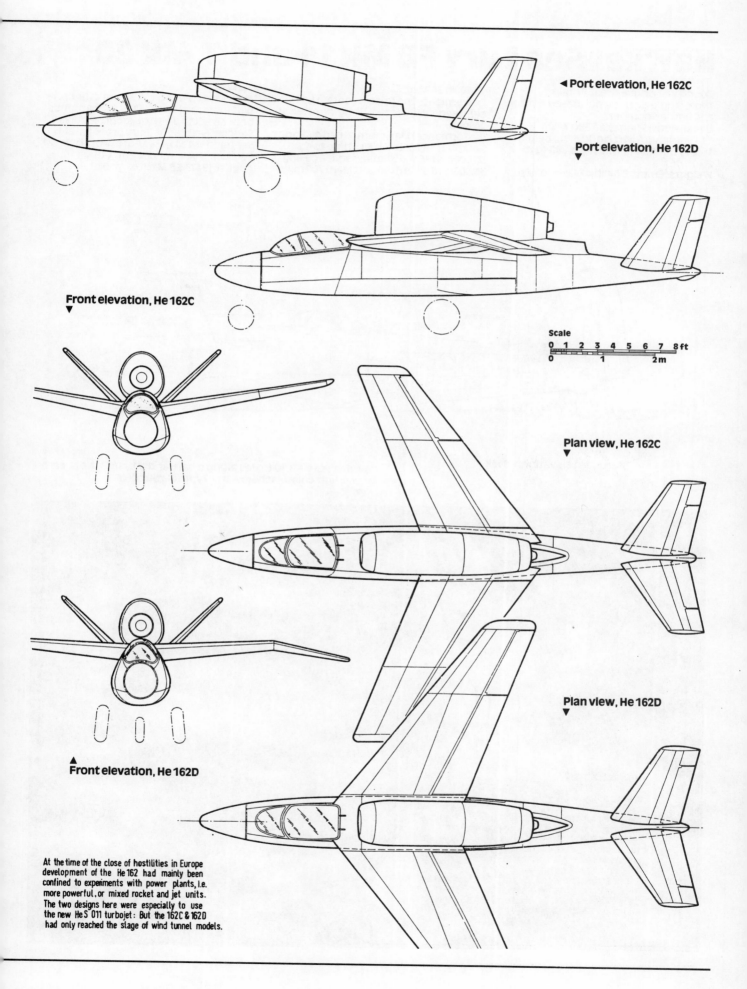

◄ Port elevation, He 162C

Port elevation, He 162D
▼

Front elevation, He 162C
▼

Scale

0	1	2	3	4	5	6	7	8 ft
0			1			2m		

Plan view, He 162C
▼

Plan view, He 162D
▼

▲
Front elevation, He 162D

At the time of the close of hostilities in Europe development of the He 162 had mainly been confined to experiments with power plants, i.e. more powerful, or mixed rocket and jet units. The two designs here were especially to use the new HeS 011 turbojet: But the 162C & 162D had only reached the stage of wind tunnel models.

Hawker Sea Fury FB Mk 11 and T Mk 20

Country of origin: Great Britain.
Type: Single-seat, carrier-based fighter and fighter-bomber.
Dimensions: Wing span 38ft 4¾in *11.70m*; length 34ft 8in *10.57m*; height 15ft 10½in *4.84m*; wing area 280 sq ft *26.01m²*.
Weights: Empty 9240lb *4192kg*; loaded

12,500lb *5672kg*.
Powerplant: One Bristol Centaurus 18 eighteen-cylinder radial engine rated at 2480hp.
Performance: Maximum speed 460mph *741kph* at 18,000ft *5485m*; time to 30,000ft *9145m*, 10.8min; service ceiling 35,800ft *10,910m*; range (clean) 700 miles

1130km.
Armament: Four fixed 20mm cannon, plus (optional) two 1000lb *454kg* bombs or twelve 60lb *27kg* rocket projectiles.
Service: First flight (Fury prototype) 1 September 1944, (Sea Fury prototype) 21 February 1945; service entry (F Mk 10) August 1947, (FB Mk II) May 1948.

Scale
0 1 2 3 4 5 6 7 8 ft
0 1 2 m

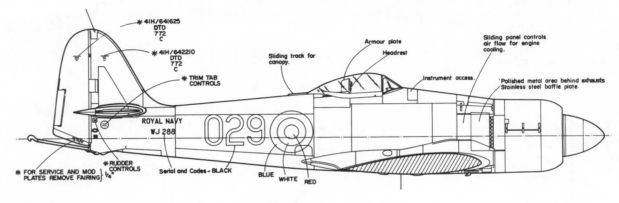

Starboard elevation, FB Mk 11

A Sea Fury FB.10 taxies along a carrier deck, 1949. Note early postwar colour scheme and Type 'C' roundels.

Port elevation, FB Mk 11
▼

Flush fasteners.

Access hatch for oil tank and Coffman starter.

Gyro gun-sight

Handhold

3" yellow arrows.

✱DO NOT STAND ON RAIL

Emergency hood release.

Colour division line

Aerial

Access panel

Static balance

Bias trim tab

Arresting hook

✱JACK HERE
↓ –1" black arrow

Wheel-forward retracting.
Tyre – 4½" wide.

ROYAL NAVY
WJ 288

029

✱TRESTLE HERE

✱HOOD JETTISON BREAK WINDOW PULL RELEASE.

Sliding canopy emergency access, ring is yellow with black stripes.

1" wide black strip.

Retractable 'footstep'

Pivoting 'footstep' for pilot access.

This blister only on some late aircraft.

Hook for carrier catapult.

Sliding gill.

A B C D E F G H I J K L

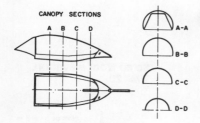

▲
Fuselage cross-sections

A B C D E F G H I J K L

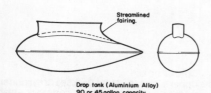

CANOPY SECTIONS

A B C D

A-A
B-B
C-C
D-D

▲
Canopy details, FB Mk 11

Streamlined fairing.

Drop tank (Aluminium Alloy) 90 or 45 gallon capacity.

▲
Scrap views
Drop tank

Sea Furies fought with distinction in the Korean War, and the FAA Historic Flight's preserved FB.11 typifies the colour scheme carried at that time.
▼

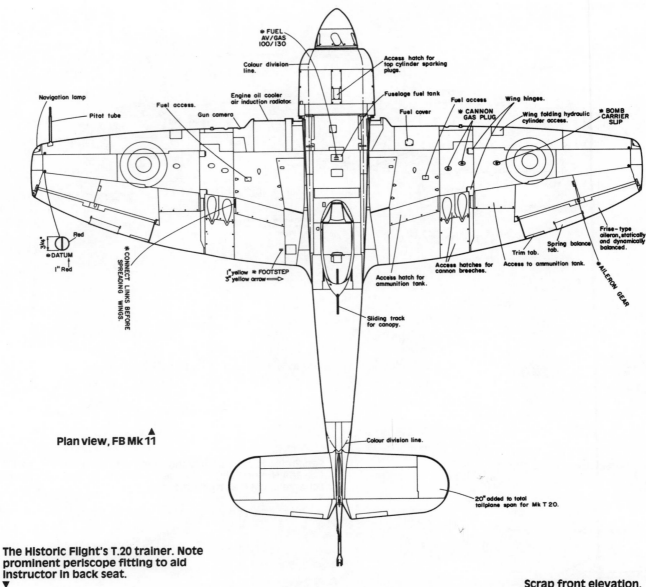

* FUEL AV/GAS 100/130

Colour division line.

Access hatch for top cylinder sparking plugs.

Engine oil cooler air induction radiator.

Fuselage fuel tank

Navigation lamp

Fuel access.

Pitot tube

Gun camera

Fuel cover

Fuel access

Wing hinges.

* CANNON GAS PLUG

Wing folding hydraulic cylinder access.

* BOMB CARRIER SLIP

3¾"   Red

* DATUM

1" Red

* CONNECT LINKS BEFORE SPREADING WINGS.

Frise – type aileron, statically and dynamically balanced.

Spring balance tab.

Trim tab.

Access to ammunition tank.

Access hatches for cannon breeches.

Access hatch for ammunition tank.

1" yellow   * FOOTSTEP
3" yellow arrow ⟹

* AILERON GEAR

Sliding track for canopy.

Plan view, FB Mk 11 ▲

Colour division line.

20" added to total tailplane span for Mk T 20.

The Historic Flight's T.20 trainer. Note prominent periscope fitting to aid instructor in back seat.
▼

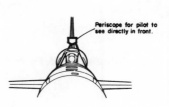

Scrap front elevation, T Mk 20
▼

Periscope for pilot to see directly in front.

Colour notes
Upper surfaces – Extra Dark Sea Grey; under surfaces – Sky. All serial nos, codes etc – Black. Stencilled markings: part nos (e.g. 41H/610358) 1in high, remainder ½in high unless shown otherwise; colour is black on Sky background and red on EDSG unless shown otherwise. All stencilling data indicated thus *.
Note: All markings except part nos appear on both sides unless indicated differently.

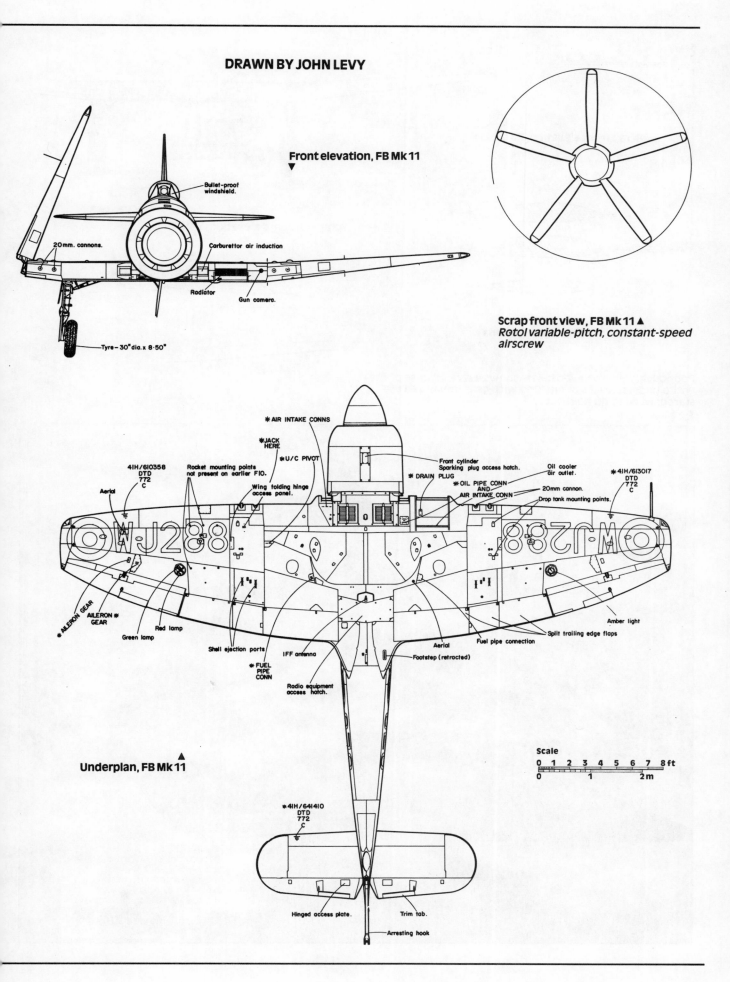

DRAWN BY JOHN LEVY

Front elevation, FB Mk 11
▼

Bullet-proof windshield.

20 mm. cannons.

Carburettor air induction

Radiator

Gun camera.

Tyre – 30" dia. x 8·50"

Scrap front view, FB Mk 11 ▲
Rotol variable-pitch, constant-speed airscrew

✱ AIR INTAKE CONNS

✱ JACK HERE

✱ U/C PIVOT

Front cylinder Sparking plug access hatch.

✱ DRAIN PLUG

Oil cooler air outlet.

✱ 4IH/6I3OI7 DTD 772 C

41H/6I0358 DTD 772 C

Rocket mounting points not present on earlier F10.

Wing folding hinge access panel.

✱ OIL PIPE CONN AND AIR INTAKE CONN

20mm cannon.

Drop tank mounting points.

Aerial

✱ ALERON GEAR

AILERON ✱ GEAR

Red lamp

Green lamp

Shell ejection ports

✱ FUEL PIPE CONN

IFF antenna

Radio equipment access hatch.

Aerial

Footstep (retracted)

Fuel pipe connection

Split trailing edge flaps

Amber light

Underplan, FB Mk 11 ▲

Scale

0 1 2 3 4 5 6 7 8 ft
0 1 2 m

✱ 4IH/64I4IO DTD 772 C

Hinged access plate.

Trim tab.

Arresting hook

Scale

0 1 2 3 4 5 6 7 8 ft
0 1 2 m

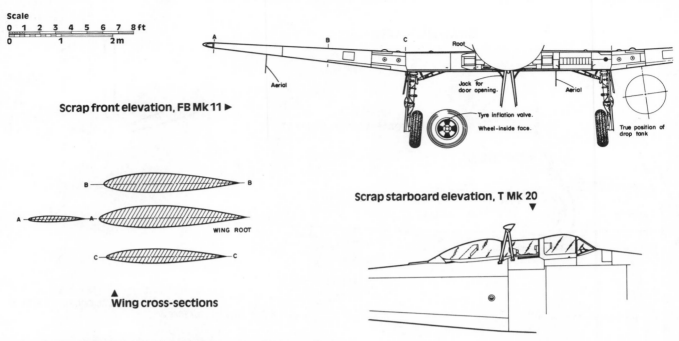

Aerial

Scrap front elevation, FB Mk 11 ▶

Root

Jack for
door opening.

Aerial

Tyre inflation valve.

Wheel-inside face.

True position of
drop tank

B ———— B

A ———— A

WING ROOT

C ———— C

▲ Wing cross-sections

Scrap starboard elevation, T Mk 20
▼

Poor quality photo nevertheless shows a rare glimpse of the entire undersurfaces of an FB.11 with gear down! Will the starboard wing tip hold out . . .?
▼

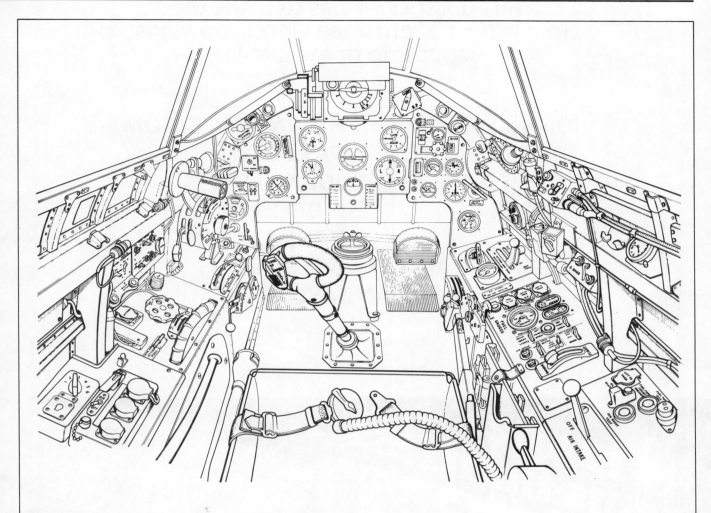

Cockpit details
By P Cooke

Key (colour notes are for TF856 but are believed to be common)

1. IFF control. 2. IFF selector unit. 3. Flare doors warning lights. 4. Flare doors operating switch. 5. Camera container master switch. 6. Rockets and bombs fusing and selection panel. 7. RATOG jettison push button. 8. Bomb rack jettison control. 9. Rudder trimming handwheel. 10. Elevator trimming handwheel (brown bakelite). 11. Cockpit (port) lamps dimmer switch. 12. Undercarriage control. 13. Arrester hook control. 14. Flaps selector unit (white knob). 15. Supercharger gear change control. 16. Fuel cut-off control (dark red knob). 17. Throttle lever. 18. RPM control lever. 19. RATOG firing button. 20. Throttle and RPM controls friction nut. 21. Canopy locking control. 22. Hydraulic handpump. 23. Sanitary bottle. 24. Arrester hook indicator light. 25. Starter re-indexing control. 26. Undercarriage position indicator. 27. Undercarriage position indicator switch. 28. Ignition switches (magnetos). 29. RI compass indicator. 30. Supercharger warning light. 31. Contacting altimeter switch. 32. Gyro gunsight selector dimmer control. 33. Ventilating louvre. 34. Gyro gunsight skid indicator. 35. Contacting altimeter. 36. Flaps position indicator. 37. Gyro gunsight. 38. Airspeed indicator. 39. Altimeter. 40. Artificial horizon. 41. Direction indicator. 42. Rate of climb indicator. 43. Turn and bank indicator. 44. Guns/RP selector switch. 45. Generator failure warning light. 46. Windscreen de-icing pump. 47. Oxygen regulator (lever in black and yellow stripes). 48.

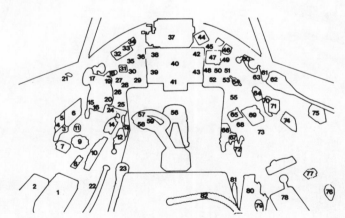

Oil pressure gauge (yellow case). 49. Engine cooling shutters control. 50. Oil temperature gauge (yellow rim). 51. Boost gauge (dark red rim). 52. Cylinder temperature gauge. 53. Engine speed indicator. 54. Canopy jettison control (black and yellow diagonal striped handle). 55. Triple pressure gauge. 56. P11 compass. 57. Press-to-speak switch. 58. Firing button. 59. Parking brake lever. 60. Sliding canopy control. 61. Safety harness locking control. 62. ZBX control unit. 63. 'Window' launcher speed control unit. 64. 'Window' launcher override control unit. 65. Main fuel cock. 66. Flaps and undercarriage emergency

selector levers (black and yellow striped knobs). Remove locking pins to operate. 67. Cockpit heating control (dark red handwheel). 68. Fuel tank air pressure gauge (pale brown rim). 69. Drop tanks jettison and selection levers (red and orange knobs respectively). 70. Mixer box. 71. VHF control unit. 72. Tailwheel locking control. 73. Engine starting buttons. 74. IFF auxiliary control unit. 75. Clock. 76. Fuel pump ammeter test socket. 77. Oil dilution pushbutton. 78. Air intake heat control. 79. Wing folding control lever. 80. Map case and chart board container. 81. Seat adjusting lever. 82. Pilot's oxygen tube.

The Publisher wishes to thank the
following draughtsmen whose drawings
appear in this volume

JOHN ALCORN   BJÖRN KARLSTRÖM
ARTHUR BENTLEY   PAT LLOYD
DOUG CARRICK   JOHN LEVY
GEORGE COX   P DELL'ORCO
R DAS   HARRY ROBINSON
GEOFF DUVAL   IAN STAIR
          BRIAN TAYLOR